The PONY EX

An Illustrated History

MW01098413

C. W. GUTHRIE

WITH PHOTOGRAPHS BY BART SMITH

TWODOT®

GUILFORD, CONNECTICUT
HELENA, MONTANA

AN IMPRINT OF GLOBE PEQUOT PRESS

Project editor: David Legere
Text design by Libby Kingsbury
Layout artist: Casey Shain
Trails map by Bob Smith, Upper West Creative Services, Helena, Montana © Morris Book Publishing, LLC

Library of Congress Cataloging-in-Publication Data is available on file.

ISBN 978-0-7627-4816-7

Printed in China

10 9 8 7 6 5 4 3 2 1

CONTENTS

Central Overland California and Pikes Peak, and Pony Express
Oregon Trail
Leavenworth and Pikes Peak Express
Smoky Hill Trail (Butterfield Overland Dispatch)
Santa Fe Trail
Butterfield Overland Mail Route (Oxbow Route)

ACKNOWLEDGMENTS

One of the many things photographer Bart Smith and I have learned while working on this book is that there are some remarkable people dedicated to keeping the spirit of the Pony Express alive and preserving the lore and the legacy. They dig through volumes of obscure records searching for historical truths. They spend countless hours examining the trails and work tirelessly to preserve what is left of the trails and stations so that future generations can trek the paths of the Pony riders. We are sincerely grateful to all of them for all they do.

We are indebted to Travis Boley of the Oregon-California Trails Association for providing materials, guidance, and cheerful advice. Travis travels the trails and truly appreciates those long-ago days. He is knowledgeable and a joy to work with. Thanks are also due to Pat Hearty and Ken Martin of the National Pony Express Association, who graciously took time to pass on their considerable knowledge, and to Chuck Milliken of the National Park Service (NPS) National Trails System Office for his words and wisdom.

Special thanks goes to Lee Kreutzer, cultural resource specialist for the NPS National Trails System Office. Lee authors the NPS National Historic Trails Auto Tour Route Interpretive Guides and generously provided us with numerous materials about the Pony Express Trail.

Applause is due Joseph Nardone of the Pony Express Trails Association for his passionate examination of details about the Pony Express and his zeal to get the history of the Pony Express right. Thanks, Joseph, for taking the time to try to set us straight.

Many thanks to Beth Anderson, whose ancestors—the David C. Bagley family— purchased and operated the Willow Springs Pony Express station, for preserving the history of the Bagley Ranch, and providing family photographs.

Our deep appreciation goes to history researcher Ann Fagre, who worked tirelessly to locate historical photographs for this book. Ann is a true professional and a pleasure to work with. We are glad to have her on our team.

On a personal note, our heartfelt thanks to Bart's lovely wife, Bridgie Graham-Smith, for holding down the home front and providing Bart the luxury of time to properly photograph the Pony Express Trail, and to my husband, Joe Guthrie, for his continued support of my writing efforts. We also thank Guy and Ann Townsend for coming up with the idea for this collaborative effort.

The Pony Express Monument in St. Joseph, Missouri.
Bart Smith

INTRODUCTION: A SPLENDID MOMENT IN HISTORY

Among the remarkable events in our nation's history that reflect the spirit and determination that forged the young United States into a great nation, there are few that captivate the world as the adventures of the daring young men of the Pony Express do. Their cherished legend has endured 150 years in books and movies and in the trails they rode, which are now preserved as the Pony Express National Historic Trail. Their ghosts haunt the plains and deserts and linger in the remaining relay stations. Each year hardy twenty-first-century Pony riders rerun the trail, keeping the spirit of those long-ago Pony Express riders alive. In 2010 the National Pony Express Association, the National Park Service, and the cities and towns along the trail will celebrate the 150th anniversary of the Pony Express—known in 1860 as the "Greatest Enterprise of Modern Times."

In the 150 years since the last Pony rider handed over the last piece of mail, the world has become high tech and high speed—we have nanosecond Internet, jet travel, fast cars, fast food, and dizzyingly fast lifestyles. The term *Pony Express,* along with *snail mail,* has become a catchword for *slow.* But in the 1860s, while the nation teetered on the brink of the Civil War, the Pony Express was the high-speed connection among the halls of Congress, the prominent cities east of the Missouri River, and the gold-rich towns 1,966 miles west in California. For that brief time in American history—the nineteen months between April 1860 and November 1861—young men riding fast horses relayed the mail between St. Joseph, Missouri, and the rapidly growing towns of Sacramento and San Francisco, California. They crossed the nearly two thousand miles of plains, deserts, and mountains in the inconceivable speed of ten days—less than half the time ever recorded for such a feat. "Think of that for perishable horse and human flesh and blood to do!" wrote Mark Twain in *Roughing It,* after watching a galloping Pony Express rider streak by the window of the Butterfield Overland stagecoach he was riding to Nevada. The Pony rider rode as if the fate of the nation was in his hands—and in some respects it was.

The United States of 1860 was a nation of separate parts. Twenty-seven of the thirty-one states lay east of the Missouri River, plus Texas and Arkansas to the south. The other two states—California and Oregon—were nearly two-thirds of the continent away. Separated by vast distances, the lonely forty-niners digging for gold in California and the emigrant farmers in the backwoods of Oregon hungered for letters from their families back east. Bankers, financiers, and the gold- and trade-wealthy entrepreneurs in Sacramento and San Francisco anxiously sent and awaited parcels carrying currency, bank drafts, and business documents and chafed at the delays. The West Coast citizenry were also desperate for newspapers and dispatches from the East to tell them what was happening in Congress. The growing populations of westerners were clamoring for faster mail service than the intolerably slow mail of four weeks by sea and nearly that long by overland stage.

On the other end of the continent, a Congress eager to speed settlement in the territories and unite the continent was grappling with the threat of secession of the Southern states over the issue of slavery and was pressing for faster communication coast to coast to ensure California's and Oregon's sympathies and rich resources stayed with the Union. It was in the midst of the nation trying to come together and threatening to break apart that a splendid moment in American history was born—the era of the Pony Express.

Pony Express rider awaits his turn at Rock Creek Pony Express Station in Nebraska. Bart Smith

A wary guard keeps a watchful eye out for Indians and robbers as the stage rolls across the plains on a starlit night. In the 1850s and 1860s, stagecoaches loaded with passengers and mail crossed the great expanse in about twenty-five to thirty days.

Old Stage-Coach of the Plains painting by Fredric S. Remington, 1901, oil on canvas, 40¼ x 27¼ inches. Courtesy Amon Carter Museum, Fort Worth, Texas

1

CONQUERING THE GREAT EXPANSE

Could young men riding fast horses relay the mail some two thousand punishing miles over the hostile terrain of the American West in often brutally harsh weather in ten days—week after week, year after year? The idea was incredible, some thought impossible. But William Hepburn Russell, the risk-taking grandee of the Russell, Majors, and Waddell freighting empire, thought it was possible and set out to prove it. His partners Alexander Majors and William Waddell had serious doubts, but, as they had all of their lives, they tackled this new challenge with fearless determination. The saga of Russell, Majors, and Waddell began thirteen years earlier.

Born in Vermont in 1812, Russell moved to western Missouri in 1828, when he was sixteen. The ambitious boy immediately went to work clerking in the Ely and Curtis store in Liberty, Missouri. Historians differ on whether Russell then went to work for the mercantile firm of James Gull and Samuel Ringo or for the Aull Brothers, who at the time were the largest business enterprise in western Missouri. Both firms had branches in Liberty and were headquartered in Lexington, Missouri. In either case, his employer recognized his skill as a merchant, and he was transferred to their headquarters in Lexington, where he eventually was made manager. By age twenty-five Russell had started his own mercantile business, and by the time he was in his thirties, he had become one of Lexington's most prominent citizens. He was president of an insurance company, had shares in the city's expansion tract, served as treasurer of Lafayette County and as Lexington's postmaster, and owned three thousand

William Hepburn Russell, the optimistic, high-stakes deal maker of the company, was the blue blood of the frontier. He reveled in the trappings and comforts of wealth. Russell was always immaculately groomed and barbered and carried himself with the bearing of a nobleman. (He actually was the descendant of Lord William Russell, who was beheaded in 1683 for plotting against Charles II.)

acres of farmland and a twenty-room mansion. But Russell was not a man to sit back and enjoy his accomplishments. He was a high-stakes risk taker who came up with new ideas for business ventures as often as the clock turned. In 1847 he ventured into the lucrative freighting business.

In the 1840s and until the first railway crossed the continent in 1869, the miles-long columns of wagons, drawn by mules or oxen and carrying food, cloth, machinery, tools, and feed for animals, were vital lifelines to the emerging settlements on the frontier and to the military posts that dotted the great expanse from the Mississippi River to the West Coast. Barring accidents on the trail—spoiled freight, Indian attacks, disease, and sudden wagon-wrecking, animal-destroying floods and snowstorms, the freighting business could turn a handsome profit.

In 1847 Russell teamed up with E. C. McCarty to transport a wagon train of goods over the Santa Fe Trail to the town of Santa Fe. Brigadier General Stephen W. Kearny had just claimed Santa Fe as a territory of the United States on his march to California during the Mexican-American War, and the shipment was not without risk. But there were no problems and the profits were sizeable, so they sent another train the following year.

In 1848 the two-year war with Mexico was over and the territories of California, Nevada, and Utah, and parts of Arizona, Wyoming, Colorado, and New Mexico were added to the lands owned by the United States. The military posts that guarded this vast territory stretched the supply lines beyond the army's capacity to haul the food, feed, weapons, and ammunition to these frontier outposts. The army quartermaster's solution was to contract with civilians to freight the army provisions.

Russell took note of the profits then being garnered by men freighting for the army and went after a chunk of that business. He formed another partnership, this time with James Brown, a seasoned freighter who had been the first to contract with the army to haul supplies in 1848. The partnership of Russell and Brown won the prized army contract to deliver supplies over the Santa Fe route. The $150,000 performance bond for the Russell and Brown army contract was signed by fellow Lexington businessman and Russell's future partner, William Bradford Waddell.

Waddell was born in Virginia of Scot ancestry and raised in Kentucky. He left home in 1824 at age seventeen. A stern, often dour plodder, he worked his way up the prosperity ladder in the Illinois lead mines, doing some farming, then at dry goods stores in St. Louis and Kentucky and

William Bradford Waddell was the penny-pinching business manager of the Russell, Majors, and Waddell partnership. The conservative Waddell and the adventuresome William Russell had many a row over Russell's wheeling and dealing. Nevertheless, Waddell remained a loyal friend and business partner. Courtesy The St. Joseph Museums, Inc., St. Joseph, Missouri

Alexander Majors was the trail-wise manager of operations in the field. He was kind to the oxen, honest and fair with his employees, and concerned himself with the moral well-being of his men. Courtesy the St. Joseph Museums, Inc., St. Joseph, Missouri

finally in Lexington. In 1835, at age twenty-eight, he opened a dry goods store on the waterfront, eventually building a hemp warehouse and operating a vigorous business in farm commodities and outfitting miners on their way to the goldfields in California. A cautious investor and a tight-fisted businessman, he acquired a moderate fortune.

Two years after Waddell signed the performance bond for Russell's venture into freighting for the army, Brown, Russell's partner, died of typhoid. The following year Russell and Waddell formed a partnership to haul military supplies to Fort Riley, Kansas, and to Fort Union, New Mexico.

Russell and Waddell's freighting business was only one of several companies delivering goods to settlements and military posts on the frontier of the early 1850s. Among the numerous freighting companies was an independent operator said to be the foremost freighter west of Missouri—Alexander Majors.

Alexander Majors, a Kentuckian whose family moved to Missouri in 1819 when he was five years old, started his adult life as a Missouri farmer. In 1848, at age thirty-six, he went into the freighting business when the army began contracting with civilian companies to haul military supplies to their posts on the frontier. He purchased six wagons and ox teams and six years later was the leading freight operator in Missouri with 100 wagons, 1,200 oxen, and 120 men.

Majors was the only one of Russell's partners who actually had experienced life on the trail. Unlike Russell and Waddell, who arranged for the cargo, purchased the stock and the wagons, hired experienced teamsters, and sent them on the trail, Majors not only assembled his freight teams, he often went along as wagon master or walked beside the teams of oxen as they plodded along the trail. At night Majors sat around the campfire eating with the men and telling tales. He was one of them, a man who in his early years as a freighter learned the job firsthand and knew the hardships and perils of the trail—rugged terrain, shifting cargo, searing heat, sudden storms, flash floods, and raging rivers to ford.

Majors was known on the frontier as a devout man who practiced the teachings of the Bible. Each man he hired was required to sign a

INSTRUCTIONS

TO

WAGON -- MASTERS,

AND ALL

Employees connected with our Trains.

1st. Commence with first wagon and corral half the wagons on the right hand side the ground selected.

2d. Stop the middle wagon of the train directly opposite and not less than 20 to 25 feet from the first wagon, and corral opposite. This will make a wide gape, which is very necessary. The wagon-master should be on his feet during corraling.

3d. As it requires three men to corral a wagon, you must select an experienced hand to drive your lead team, so that when he stops he can assist the next teamsters, he being on one side, the wagon master on the other, and the teamster with his lead cattle to prevent them tangling with the team ahead. He can assist until he is released by the assistant, who must be on foot.

4th. When about corraling, caution your men against exciting the cattle, by hallooing and cracking whips at them. They should be so careful that a long, deep-toned "whoo" would stop their teams in the exact spot required.

5th. Teamsters should not commence to unyoke till their side of the corral is completed, then they will begin with the leaders and continue down to the wheelers, always loosing the chain and yoke from those yoked.

6th. If water be near the camp, let the cattle feed to it instead of being driven there. But if necessary to drive them, let them linger some time about the water, so that they all may become cool and have a chance to satisfy their thirst.

7th. See that the cattle get on the best feeding ground in the vicinity of the camp, and also that when turned out that they have a sufficient guard by day and night, and never to be left without a guard.

8th. In driving cattle to corral, men enough must be employed to encircle them and drive them directly in, and when at a distance from camp, drive them very slowly, as fast driving injures them greatly.

9th. No man should begin yoking before the cattle have had two or three minutes to become quieted in, then all should enter and yoke in a quiet gentle manner. First yoke the wheelers and chain them to the front wheel outside the corral, or hitch them to the tongue; secondly, yoke the leaders and fasten them to the wagon, on the inside; then the yoke next the leaders, and so on till the whole team is yoked and hitched up, when they will be taken out of the corral and hitched to the wagon.

10th. While yoking a man must be in the front gap, and two or three in the hind one. If not required at the gaps, the wagon master must be instructing the teamsters how to yoke with the greatest facility.

11th. After leaving corral, do not travel more than 1-2 to 1 mile before stopping 8 or 10 minutes for the cattle to breathe and urinate, particularly if the [illegible] When you have selected a capable hand to lead the train, always keep him as leader, and if all the teamsters keep the place they had when starting, they soon learn in what way to manage their teams, and the teams soon learn the art of corraling.

12th. When traveling or corraling every man must keep a strict observance to the password, so that if any accident occurs in the train the whole train may be notified at once, and all assistance rendered that is necessary.

13th. Drive the oxen into the corral in the morning as soon as the teamsters can see to yoke, and travel till about 10 A. M., varying an hour more or less, according to camping ground. Remain in camp 2 or 3 hours, and then make the evening drive. These rules are for conducting a loaded train.

14th. The same rules may be observed in an empty train, in regard to hitching up as early as you can see, but in this case travel until 7 or 9 o'clock A. M., according the time of getting off.—As a general thing an empty train should not travel more than from 6 to 8 miles; and a loaded train from 7 to 10, according to camping ground. The hands should cook and eat in such time as to enable the train to hitch up again in an hour and a half to two hours, when you will make another drive of from 6 to 8 miles, and then remain in camp 3 to 4 hours, as this is the warm part of the day, and this will give animals and men a chance to rest; then hitch up, always taking your stoutest cattle for the teams, and make an evening drive, which will sometimes throw you a little after dark in coming to camp. When arrived turn out your cattle, put out your guard, and let the rest of the hands go to bed. This will give hands two meals a day, which is sufficient for men on the plains, as they eat hearty and have strong diet.

15th. Before starting see that the lock chains are properly wrapped, so as to prevent cutting the spokes, and to keep them so during the whole trip you should provide yourself with suitable gunny sacks before starting.

16th. Keep your wagon well greased, as a failure in this oftentimes ruins boxes; also, once a week, if not oftener, have a little grease put in the hook of each ox chain, in the goose-neck of the tongue, and in the yoke staples which have rings.

17th. Do not allow the men to whip their teams at all. The use of profane language is strictly forbidden. We expect our trains to observe the Sabbath, and whenever an opportunity occurs to hear preaching, embrace it. We want our men to pay due respect to all persons they meet on the road, whether Indians or whites, as many difficulties often occur from abuse and insult offered to inoffensive people.

18th. The wagon master must see that all his orders are obeyed promptly and exactly as given; if this is the case he will be respected, and it is our wish that he should see that the hands cultivate a feeling of self respect and friendship, that nothing but the kindest feeling may exist among them. This is necessary for the well-being of every body of men associated together promiscuously as they are with trains on the plains.

19th. You will see by these rules that loaded trains ought to travel from 15 to 18 miles per day, the weather being ordinarily good, this being done in [illegible] returning trains should travel from 18 to 21 miles per day in ordinary good weather, this being done in three drives, as heretofore stated.

20th. We will add that the statements made above are facts that have come under our personal observation during an experience of several years on the plains, and we know them to be of indispensable importance, and that they must be strictly obeyed in order to follow the plains with any success.

RUSSELL, MAJORS & WADDELL.

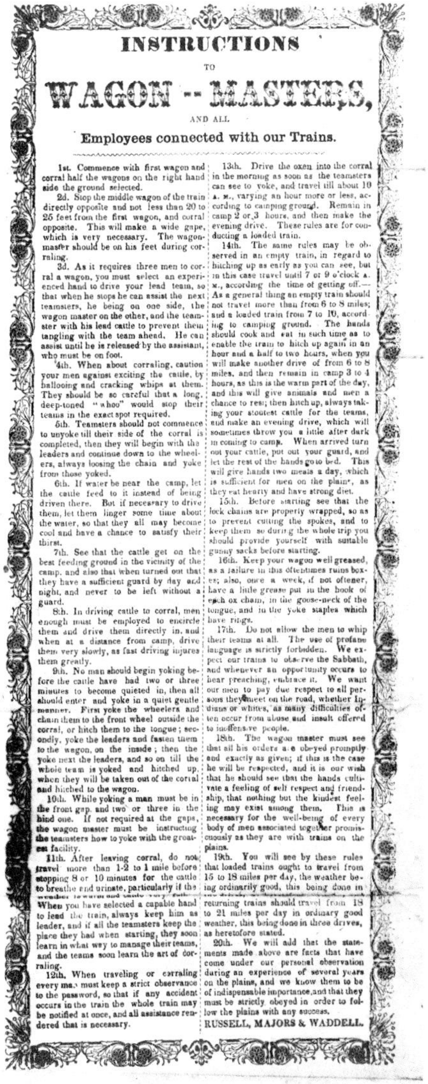

Major's instructions to his teamsters on how they were to care for the oxen seemed pious but proved practical—fewer animals died along the trail. This item is reproduced by permission of The Huntington Library, San Marino, California.

The Passage of the "Enabling Act of Kansas Territory" brought many Settlers throu

pledge that promised, "While I am in the employ of A. Majors I agree not to use profane language, not to get drunk, not to gamble, not to treat animals cruelly, and not to do anything else that is incompatible with the conduct of a gentleman. And I agree, if I violate any of the above conditions, to accept my discharge without any pay for my services."

er Gateways – 1854

A fast-moving stagecoach passes a line of wagons drawn by plodding oxen headed west.

Kansas State Historical Society

He ordered his teamsters to rest the oxen and themselves on Sundays. According to David Nevin and other historians of the Old West, Majors's insistence on observing the Sabbath was a joke on the frontier, but customers and competing freight companies soon realized that his rested teams made their deliveries in record time, earning him large profits and more contracts, and his honesty and fairness won him the respect of hard-bitten teamsters.

By 1854 the army was weary of the logistical nightmare of contracting with the sixteen or so different freighting companies that delivered their supplies. They sent out the word that the following year they would award a single contract for two years (previously contracts were issued for one year). At the time, no single freighting company had the wagons, oxen, men, or capital or credit to acquire enough to fulfill such a contract, but two freighting companies might. In January 1855 Russell and Waddell merged with their rival in the freighting business, Majors.

The three men were opposites in bent, background, and strengths, and each took the role best suited to him. Russell was a genius at promoting deals and had a wide range of business and political connections. Waddell kept a watchful eye on costs and a skeptical eye on income and oversaw the day-to-day business details. Majors manned, organized, and ramrodded operations on the trail. They built their headquarters in Kansas, near the quartermaster depot at Fort Leavenworth, and set up operations.

The partnership of Russell, Majors, and Waddell became the largest and most famous freighting company in the West, with five hundred wagons, seventy-five hundred oxen, and seventeen hundred men. Their miles-long trains of Conestoga wagons pulled by plodding oxen wound their way across the prairies, deserts, and mountains. They delivered food, cloth, machinery, tools, and grain for animals to settlements and food, feed, and weaponry to military posts that dotted the American West of the 1850s and early 1860s.

The firm earned handsome profits in its first two years of operation, but in 1857 the company suffered a half-million-dollar loss. The army contracted with Russell, Majors, and Waddell to haul three million pounds of supplies to the army expedition that had been sent to Utah to quell the Mormons' defiance of federal authority. Such a shipment nearly equaled their shipments for a full year and far exceeded the company's capacity. Additional wagons and oxen would have to be purchased and additional men hired, and the wagon trains would

be at risk not only from hostile Indians but also from angry Mormons. The army insisted, promising that although contractors ordinarily bore the losses they incurred on the trail, that for this shipment the company would be reimbursed.

About seventy miles beyond South Pass, Wyoming, a Mormon party under the command of Major Lot Smith attacked the wagon trains, burned the wagons and supplies, and drove off most of the oxen. What was left of the wagon trains met with more trouble—Cheyenne Indians stole the beef cattle, Mormons stole nine hundred more oxen, and a severe snowstorm claimed the rest. The loss to the company of nearly half a million dollars exceeded their first two years' profits. They billed the government and anxiously awaited payment—which they would never receive. Three years later the government advised them that since there was no written agreement, they could not honor the claim.

Leaping into the Overland Mail and Passenger Service

In the same year that Russell, Majors, and Waddell suffered that devastating financial loss, Congress voted for a $600,000 subsidy for a semiweekly overland mail and passenger service from the Mississippi River to San Francisco. Largely as a result of the loud voices of southern politicians proclaiming the central overland route's Rocky Mountains could not be crossed in winter, and the decision of the postmaster general Aaron Brown, a proslavery Tennessean, the route through the South was chosen. It had two eastern terminals—Memphis and St. Louis—then went to Fort Smith, Arkansas, and bowed southward through Oklahoma, Texas, and along the southern borders of U.S. territory. Dubbed the "oxbow" route, the twenty-eight-hundred-mile stage and mail line was a thousand miles longer than the central overland route. The six-year contract was awarded to John Butterfield, who controlled most of the eastern stage lines and together with Henry Wells and William Fargo founded the American Express Company in 1850. He named the about-to-be-famous stage line the Butterfield Overland Express Company.

In 1858, while Russell, Majors, and Waddell grappled with their financial losses, gold was discovered in present-day Colorado, and miners rushed to make claims and build camps between Pikes Peak and Longs Peak. The Pikes Peak gold rush of 1858 was expected to equal the California gold rush ten years earlier. Hoping to capitalize on the rush of prospectors and settlers to the Pikes Peak goldfields, Russell immediately began organizing a stage and mail line to run between Leavenworth and Denver. Majors and Waddell refused to join him on this venture. Russell convinced John S. Jones, a former freighter, and Luther R. Smoot, his former banking partner in the firm of Smoot, Russell & Co., to invest in the enterprise. Russell's eldest son, John, was secretary, and Benjamin F. Ficklin, who had worked for Russell, Majors, and Waddell in the freighting business, was named general manager and would later be the general superintendent of the Pony Express. The optimistic partners laid out the 680-mile road between Leavenworth and the gold diggings, purchased fifty-two Concord coaches and eight hundred mules to pull them, outfitted twenty-seven stage stations along the way, and hired 108 men to operate the stages and the stations. They named their stage and mail service the Leavenworth City and Pikes Peak Express Company, or L. & P. P. Express Co.

The Pikes Peak "diggings" were a monumental disappointment, and Russell's hoped-for influx of prospectors and resulting revenue from the stage and mail service never materialized. In 1859, deeper in debt but undaunted, Russell's L. & P. P. Express Co., on the strength of promissory notes, purchased John Hockaday's semimonthly

By Sea to California

Before overland mail routes spanned the continent, all freight and mail from the eastern states bound for California went by ship. There were two shipping routes—the thirteen-thousand-mile, three-month trip around the tip of South America and the six-thousand-mile, twenty-eight-day Panama shortcut. As the population of California and the demand for mail service increased, the U.S. Post Office Department issued a contract in 1848 to the Pacific Mail Steamship Company to carry the mail from New York to California. At first parcels were delivered by ship to Panama, then across the isthmus by canoe and mule pack, and then loaded onto another ship to San Francisco. In 1855, when the Panama Railroad was completed, the mail crossed the isthmus by train. The ocean mail contracts expired in 1860.

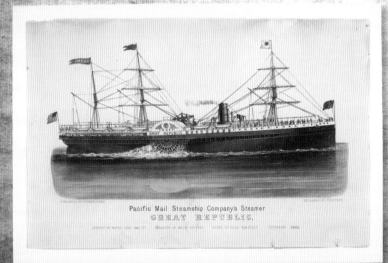

Pacific Mail Steamship Company's Steamer
GREAT REPUBLIC.

Lithograph by Currier & Ives. Courtesy The Bancroft Library, University of California, Berkeley, California

Ships like this Pacific Mail Steamship Company's steamer **The Great Republic** *brought freight and mail from the East Coast of the United States to the West Coast until 1860.*

contract to carry the U.S. mail between St. Joseph, Missouri, and Salt Lake City by way of Fort Kearny, Fort Laramie, and Fort Bridger. On the heels of the Hockaday purchase, Russell bought out George Chorpenning's contract to transport mail between Salt Lake City and Sacramento. Thus on the stroke of a pen and a promise, Russell's L. & P. P. Express Co. owned the central overland mail delivery service from the Missouri River to California.

Both Hockaday and Chorpenning had transported the mail by pack mule, known disparagingly on the frontier as the "jackass" mail. When Russell's L. & P. P. Express Co. took over, it transported the mail by stagecoach. The company had already stopped its coach service to Denver and diverted the men, coaches, and stock to the route to Salt Lake City. Russell spent lavishly buying more Concord coaches, paying top dollar for mules and fine horses, building more way stations along the route, and hiring more men to operate the extensive stage and mail service from St. Joseph to Sacramento. By mid-October 1859 the L. & P. P. Express Co. had its stage line up and running and providing excellent service. Unfortunately, Russell's premier stage and mail line was running at a daily financial loss, and the company was over half a million dollars in debt.

Grabbing a Bear by the Tail

Russell turned to his freight business partners, Majors and Waddell, to bail the stage and mail company out. They had little choice. Much of the credit Russell had received to develop the service was on the strength of the exemplary reputation of the firm of Russell, Majors, and Waddell. Their company's reputation was at stake, and such honorable men as Majors and Waddell could not ignore Russell's plight. They took over the financially troubled stage line and refinanced its debts. The new stage line was incorporated under the name of the Central Overland California and Pikes Peak Express Company.

Majors and Waddell put their significant management skills to work, but despite their vigorous efforts they could not turn the stage and mail line into a moneymaker. In January 1860 Russell took a huge gamble to save the company. He was in Washington on one of his many trips to hobnob with politicians and businessmen. The capital was abuzz with the talk of war and the almost-certain Southern secession from the Union and what to do about it. Senator William McKendree Gwin of California and many Northerners were rightly concerned that the primary overland mail route from Washington to the West was Butterfield's Oxbow line through the South, which could easily be cut off by Southern troops. A faster mail and dispatch service than the twenty-five days by Butterfield coach (Butterfield's best ever time was twenty-one days) was also critical if the Union was to counter Southern sympathies in the gold and resource-rich West Coast states of California and Oregon and keep them in the Union. The advantages of the more direct, thousand-miles shorter central overland route were obvious. The only question was whether the mail could dependably be transported in winter over the Sierra Nevada Mountains. Following a conversation with Gwin, Russell, as was his character, plunged headlong into a new enterprise. On January 27, 1860, he sent a telegram to Leavenworth to John W. Russell, his son and business associate in the stage line:

> HAVE DETERMINED TO ESTABLISH A PONY EXPRESS TO SACRAMENTO, CALIFORNIA, COMMENCING 3RD OF APRIL. TIME TEN DAYS.

According to Majors in his memoir, *Seventy Years on the Frontier*, and Christopher Corbett's *Orphans Preferred*, when Russell returned from Washington he told Majors and Waddell that if their company could demonstrate that the central route could continue to operate in winter, Gwin had vowed to use his considerable influence to get a subsidy to pay the expenses of such an undertaking. Russell had given his word to Gwin, and in so doing, the word of his partners Majors and Waddell. Their given word was sacred to men of their substance and as good as a bond. As one historian put it, "Majors and Waddell had a bear by the tail and couldn't let go." Russell had committed them to a monumental undertaking, and they had a short two months to set up a horse relay operation to carry the mail nearly two thousand miles, part of which was over the treacherous Sierra Nevada and Rocky Mountains, in ten days. Majors and Waddell and the indomitable Russell called in their best men and went to work organizing what was later to be heralded as the "Greatest Enterprise of Modern Times"—the Pony Express.

2

YOUNG MEN AND MUSTANGS

The maiden run of the Pony Express was scheduled for April 3, 1860, two months and a few days after Russell sent his telegraph announcing his decision and convincing his partners to go along with him on the spectacular and risky venture that could make or break them—speeding the mail across two-thirds of the continent in ten days.

The decision was made. Russell, Majors, and Waddell and the men they hired had just sixty-seven days to put in place horses, riders, stations, feed, and equipment and organize a 1,966-mile mail-relay operation. Moreover, they had to do it during the time when the very reason for the Pony Express was the intolerably slow twenty-one to twenty-five days it took to communicate between the East and the West.

The trail of the Pony Express followed nearly the same track as the old Oregon Trail from St. Joseph to Fort Bridger, then dropped southwest, taking the old Mormon and California trails to Salt Lake and due west to Sacramento and San Francisco. Russell set up operations in St. Joseph and arranged the mail connections from New York, Washington, D.C., and points east to the St. Joe Pony Express headquarters. Benjamin Ficklin, the general superintendent of the Central Overland California and Pikes Peak Express Company, was also in charge of Pony Express field operations from Missouri to the West Coast.

The Coming and Going of the Pony Express painting by Fredric S. Remington. Courtesy Gilcrease Museum, Tulsa, Oklahoma

The success of the Pony Express's ten-day schedule hung on the courage and dependability of the young riders carrying the mail and the speed and stamina of the horses they rode.

The Virginian

Adventurer Benjamin Franklin Ficklin was known on the frontier as a no-nonsense, tough-as-nails leader of men. But beneath the surface lurked a fun-loving prankster who relished nonsense. Born in Albemarle County, Virginia, in 1827, Ficklin, a preacher's son, entered the Virginia Military Institute (VMI) in 1844 to, as one historian put it, be tamed and educated. Young Ficklin ranked low in academics, low in military decorum, and legendary in pranks. During his first two years at VMI, he buried school superintendent Frances H. Smith's boots in a snowbank, painted Smith's horse white with red stripes, and ignited a string of firecrackers under the reviewing stand during a Fourth of July dress parade. One night in November 1846, he snuck out to the parade grounds, put a charge of powder in the school's howitzer, aimed it at the cadet barracks, and fired. The powder charge was larger than he figured; the blast blew out the windows in the barracks and rattled Lexington. This last prank was more than Smith could tolerate. He summarily expelled Ficklin.

Rather than endure his father's wrath, Ficklin went to war. He joined the army and fought in the war with Mexico, earning the rank of corporal and

Benjamin Franklin Ficklin
The Museum of the Confederacy,
Richmond, Virginia

receiving a minor wound. After his discharge he returned to VMI and insisted he be reinstated by planting himself on Smith's office steps and refusing to budge until Smith relented. Smith apparently admired the young soldier's grit and let him return. Ficklin graduated in 1849 fourth from the bottom of the class. Upon receiving his diploma he ceremoniously skewered it on his bayonet and marched triumphantly from the hall.

Ficklin taught school for a short period, found it dull, and went west in the early 1850s to work for Russell, Majors, and Waddell's freighting company. In 1857 he had enough of freighting and longed for a little excitement. He found it as a courier and scout for Colonel Albert Sidney Johnston's expedition during the Mormon War. Three years later he was working for Russell's Central Overland California and Pikes Peak Express Company as general superintendent.

Three months after Ficklin had organized the operations of the Pony Express, he was off on another adventure, teaming up with Jeptha Wade and Hiram Sibley to install the telegraph line between the East and the West—which ironically would halt the Pony Express operation he had just set up.

Five months before the transcontinental telegraph lines were connected, Ficklin was back in Virginia as a major in the Confederate Army. He served briefly as the quartermaster general of the Virginia State Volunteers, then wrangled an assignment to fight in the field. Ficklin not only survived the Seven Days Battles near Richmond, he came out a hero after rescuing a cannon from the Union. Plagued by asthma Ficklin was forced to take a desk job and sent to England to buy war materials for the Confederacy.

A month before Lee's surrender at Appomattox, the Confederacy sent Ficklin to Washington to see President Lincoln. While he waited for an audience, Lincoln was assassinated. A telegraph operator, for unknown reasons, became suspicious and reported Ficklin to the authorities, describing him as "about six feet tall, dark hair, cut short, sallow complexion, long thin nose, small black eyes, well back in his head and thin features, altogether more muscle than flesh, as a whole presenting the appearance of a refined pirate." Ficklin was arrested on April 16 while walking down Pennsylvania Avenue, spent a couple of months in jail, and then finally was cleared of charges of complicity in the assassination of Lincoln.

Ficklin took the oath of allegiance to the United States and returned to Virginia—but not for long. In 1867 he went to Texas to start a stage and mail service between San Antonio and El Paso. Four years later Ficklin and his partner were in Washington to sign the mail contracts for the coming year. During dinner at the Willard Hotel, a fish bone became lodged in Ficklin's throat. While the doctor was trying to remove the bone, the forceps slipped and cut into an artery. On March 10, 1871, Benjamin Ficklin, who was in the thick of every significant event of the 1840s through the 1860s—War with Mexico, overland freight and stage travel, the Pony Express, the telegraph, the Civil War, and Lincoln's assassination—bled to death.

Planning the Route

Ficklin, along with A. B. Miller, a partner of Russell's in a merchandising business, and James Bromley, the superintendent of operations for Russell's former L. & P. P. Express Co., planned the route and determined the number of stations, horses, and riders necessary. They divided the route into five divisions: Division One—St. Joseph, Missouri, to Fort Kearny, Nebraska; Division Two—Platte station to Horseshoe Creek, Wyoming; Division Three—Elkhorn to Salt Lake City, Utah; Division Four—Trader's Rest to Roberts Creek, Nevada; and Division Five—Camp

station to Sacramento and San Francisco, California. Bromley took over as superintendent of Division Three, and they hired four other men they could count on to serve as division superintendents—A. E. Lewis, the outlaw Joseph Slade, Howard Egan, and Boliver Roberts. The division superintendents hired riders and saw to it that the existing stage stations on the trail were ready and that new ones were built where required. They hired station keepers and wranglers to take care of the horses and arranged with local merchants to deliver equipment, tools, supplies, and food and feed for the animals to the stations. It was their task to have the horses and riders in place and to supervise operations once the service was up and running.

The Stations

The Pony Express used the existing stage stations along the route wherever possible and built additional home and relay stations where they were needed. Stations were located the distance apart that a fast horse could run at a full gallop before tiring and beginning to slow and the rider needed a fresh mount to maintain the pace. The first relay stations were about twenty-five miles apart. When it became obvious that even the

Ruby Valley Pony Express Station. Bart Smith

best horses could not maintain their top speed for that long a distance, more relay stations were built to shorten the distance between changes of horses—generally fifteen miles on prairies and deserts where the ground was relatively flat, and eight to ten miles in the mountains. If the site was not near a natural source of water, the station was built anyway and water freighted in by the nearest merchant, along with the feed for the horses and food for the station keepers and Pony riders.

The relay stations made no pretense at being other than a two-minute stop to change horses. The station keepers' quarters were built from whatever materials were handy—timber where it was available, sod in Kansas and Nebraska, adobe in the deserts. In the barren lands some relay stations were little more than a dugout carved into a hillside and roofed with logs that had been freighted in. In all, there were 184 stations along the trail. Twenty-five were home stations for changing riders, and 159 relay stations, also known as "swing" stations, were for changing horses. According to Joseph J. DiCerto in *The Saga of the Pony Express,* at least four of the relay stations were sometimes used as home stations.

Running a remote relay station was a hard living for station keepers. Some were mere sod huts or dugouts with timber roofs; others were solid-built adobe or log structures. Pity the men assigned to the sod huts and dugouts. Food, feed, water, and firewood were scarce and stingily managed. Attacks by robbers and Indians were common. Pony riders who were there only long enough to jump off one horse, throw the mail pouch over the saddle of a fresh one, gulp a drink of water, maybe grab a biscuit from the outstretched hand of a station keeper, and gallop away, left the station keepers and stock tenders to go about rounding up food, feed, water, and wood, tending to the horses, and waiting for the momentary excitement of the next rider's arrival.

After changing horses at four to seven relay stations and riding seventy-five to one hundred miles, riders thankfully pulled their pony up to a home station, passed the mail onto the next rider, and headed into the station house for a meal and a bunk. Home stations were generally a rung above relay stations in comfort, which gave the rider some ease, some conversation, maybe a card game, and a little "medicinal" whiskey before he had to go out on the trail again.

The Riders

> ### WANTED
> —YOUNG, SKINNY, WIRY FELLOWS,
> NOT OVER EIGHTEEN.
> MUST BE EXPERT RIDERS, WILLING TO RISK
> DEATH DAILY.
> ORPHANS PREFERRED. WAGES $25 A WEEK.
> APPLY, CENTRAL OVERLAND EXPRESS,
> ALTA BLDG., MONTGOMERY ST.

Few if any of the Pony Express riders were orphans, and most were over eighteen. This most popular myth about Pony Express riders came from an article in a 1923 *Sunset* magazine and somehow has endured as a provocative image of the riders. According to Pony Express author Christopher Corbett, "We can be reasonably certain they were daring, expert riders, willing to risk death daily. But they were probably not orphans."

Orphaned or not, it was an extraordinary bunch of young men eager for adventure and the good pay of $50 to $150 a month, depending on the distance and risk of their run, plus bed and board, who flocked to St. Joseph, Salt Lake City, and Sacramento to try out for the Pony Express. Hundreds came to show their ability with a horse. Eighty were signed on. (Eventually more riders were hired to replace those who went into some other line of work or just couldn't take the long, punishing rides.) Pony riders had a grueling, hard, and dangerous job that would test their mettle nearly every trip. They knew it—even before they lined up to be hired for the job. Once the pouch carrying the mail from St. Joseph or Sacramento was placed in the care of a Pony Express rider, it was to never stop until it reached its final destination.

"We had to go before a justice of the peace and swear we would be at our posts at all times, and not go further than one hundred yards from the station except for carrying the mail. When we started out we were not to turn back, no matter what happened, until we had delivered the mail at the next station," wrote Pony rider Nick Wilson in his autobiography, *The White Indian Boy: The Story of Uncle Nick Among the Shoshones*. Day and night they rode, changing horses along the way and passing the mail from rider to rider. They rode through snowstorms and windstorms, across raging rivers, and over barren deserts in searing heat. They outran Indians and robbers, and when they finished a run, they had to be ready to start back at "half a minute's notice," recalled Wilson.

They were indeed a special breed—young, determined men around the age of twenty with a strong sense of responsibility and a giant measure of grit, who weighed around 125 pounds and could and would ride like the devil was on his tail hour after grueling hour.

Pony riders were not required to wear uniforms and dressed as it suited them, but they were given a bible and required to sign Majors's famous frontier pledge of loyalty, honesty, and sobriety. When the Civil War started, they also swore an oath of allegiance to the Union. At first the riders were armed with a Spencer rifle strapped across their back and two Colt revolvers in holsters on their hip. The rifle, which proved unwieldy on these high-speed rides, and one of the pistols were eventually abandoned. The rider carried one pistol in a holster or tucked into his belt. Some riders carried horns, as did some stage drivers, to signal to the relay station they were coming in.

The Horses

Bible presented to Pony Express riders.
Courtesy The Society of California Pioneers, San Francisco, California

> **WANTED**
> TWO HUNDRED GREY MARES
> FROM FOUR TO SEVEN YEARS OLD,
> NOT TO EXCEED FIFTEEN HANDS
> HIGH, WELL BROKE TO SADDLE AND
> WARRANTED SOUND,
> WITH BLACK HOOFS, AND SUITABLE FOR
> RUNNING THE OVERLAND PONEY EXPRESS
> JONES, RUSSELL & CO.
> FEB. 10, 1860, *LEAVENWORTH DAILY TIMES*

East Coast Pony Express advertisement dated July 1, 1861, publicizing reduced rates and a change of time.
Nevada Historical Society, Reno, Nevada

William Russell's flair for elegant trappings was evident in his attempt to purchase well-bred Eastern horses—grays with black hooves—for the Pony Express. How many gray mares were acquired is uncertain. Whether they were tried and then replaced as unsuitable is also not clear. In any case, William Finney, in charge of operations on the West Coast, purchased California half-breed mustangs for the rides from Sacramento to Carson City, half-wild mustangs were used on the trail from Carson City to Fort Laramie, and according to farriers and Pony riders, mustangs were used as far east as St. Joseph.

Levi Hensel, the farrier for the Pony Express in Seneca, Kansas, declared the half-wild horses were "the worst imps of Satan in the business." In Hensel's 1901 statement as reported by Frank Root and William Connelley in *The Overland Stage to California* and repeated in Christopher Corbett's *Orphans Preferred*, he went on to say, "The only way I could master them was to throw them and get a rope around each foot and stake them out, and have a man on the head and another on the body while I trimmed the feet and nailed the shoes on, and then they would squeal and bite all the time I was working on them. It generally took half a day to shoe one of them." Hensel was also quick to add that the mustangs seem to never tire and were the best and fastest horses for racing across the country.

The Pony riders tended to agree with Hensel. Riders William Campbell and Nick Wilson both claimed that the men who purchased the horses knew their business when they bought up "every mean, bucking, kicking horse that could be found, but they were good stock, and could outrun anything along the trail."

Pony rider Nick Wilson, who had lived with the Shoshoni Indians as a boy, knew the reason the Pony Express horses could outrun everything else on the trail: They were grain fed. He saw the effect when a band of Indian riders jumped him between Shell Creek and Deep Creek, Utah. "I looked back over my shoulder," Nick said, "and saw them coming, about thirteen of the devils, as hard as they could ride after me, yellin' and shootin'." But his horse had the advantage of superior feed; "the horse's grain-fed muscles got me out of the danger of their arrows and the few old guns they had. Their grass-fed ponies couldn't keep long within gunshot."

The Mail

In the early days of the Pony Express, the mail was carried in saddlebags or pouches that did not adequately protect the important mail inside them during high-speed rides, raging river crossings, and mail transfers from one horse to another. By late 1860 a specially made leather saddle apron with a hole for the horn and a slit for the cantle was used to carry the mail. Known as a *mochila* (Spanish for "knapsack"), it covered the entire saddle and had mail pockets called *cantinas* on each corner. The *mochila* was not attached to the saddle and could be yanked off one horse and thrown onto another in less than a minute. The same *mochila* was passed from rider to rider until it reached the end of the trail at St. Joseph or Sacramento.

Letters, telegrams, and newspapers were printed on special tissue-thin paper, carefully wrapped in silk oilcloth to protect them, and placed in three of the four pockets, which were then locked. Only the postal station keepers at the end of the line had keys. The front pocket on the left side was the "way pocket." It was used to carry the card that the station keeper wrote the time the rider arrived and left and held letters for riders and relay station keepers between home stations. Initially the price to deliver a letter weighing half an ounce or less was $5.00. Later the price was unexplainably dropped to $2.50. Overall the average price to deliver a letter by Pony Express was $3.00, which was a whopping loss to the company of about $16.00 per letter.

Ready to Run

By the day of the scheduled inaugural run—April 3, 1860—Russell, Majors, and Waddell, Ficklin, Finney, and the five division superintendents had masterfully arranged to have everything in place. The East and West terminals were ready to do business. A spectacular ceremony was planned in St. Joseph for the start of the run to the West. St. Joseph mayor Jeff Thompson and Majors were on hand to give speeches, and more dignitaries were on the way to witness the start of the great enterprise. Russell was there, anxious and busy running things, but didn't plan to speak. In Hannibal, Missouri, the steamer locomotive Missouri, pulling a tender and the first car specially constructed to carry mail in the United States, was readied to rush letters from Washington, D.C., and New York to St. Joseph to meet the scheduled launch of the first Pony Express rider west at 5 p.m. In San Francisco a ceremonial departure of the first Pony rider east was staged. He would depart the Alta Telegraph Office on Montgomery Street and ride to the dock where the steamer *New World* would carry the mail pouch to Sacramento, and the first rider east would gallop toward St. Joseph.

Along the trail of the Pony Express, the home and relay stations, at that time generally twenty-five miles apart (later ten to twelve miles

Charlie Cliff hired on with the Pony Express in May 1860 when he was twenty-four and stayed with the company until the Pony Express ended in November 1861. He had the run between St. Joseph, Missouri, and Seneca, Kansas. After his days with the Pony Express he drove a freight wagon. The St. Joseph Museums, Inc., St. Joseph, Missouri

apart), were manned with station keepers and stock tenders (horse wranglers) and provisioned with food, feed, and water. Four hundred to five hundred horses, mostly mustangs, were distributed along the route and stood ready, and eighty anxious riders awaited their turn to leap into the saddle.

John Burnett rode for the Pony Express, but in this photograph he looks every bit the Wells Fargo agent he later became. The St. Joseph Museums, Inc., St. Joseph, Missouri

David Jay was thirteen when he hired on to make the Pony Express run between Seneca and Big Sandy and later between Big Sandy and Fort Kearny. After his days with the Pony Express, he enlisted in the Kansas Cavalry and fought at the Battle of Westport. A jack-of-all-trades, Jay later worked for the railroad and was a policeman for a while. The St. Joseph Museums, Inc., St. Joseph, Missouri

Patrick McEneaney rode only five months with the Pony Express, then joined the U.S. Regiment of Dragoons serving ten years with the predecessor of the 1st Cavalry Regiment of the U.S. Army. The St. Joseph Museums, Inc., St. Joseph, Missouri

Painting by Charles Hargens. Courtesy The Pony Express National Museum, Inc., St. Joseph, Missouri

First westbound rider leaving St. Joseph.

3

THE RIDE THAT LAUNCHED A LEGEND

Westbound Ride into History

*I*t was 7:15 p.m. on April 3, 1860. The shadows of early evening were settling on the bustling frontier town of St. Joseph on the bend of the Missouri River. Johnny Fry, a twenty-year-old Kansas farm boy, or Johnson William "Billy" Richardson, a twenty-six-year-old Virginia seaman turned Pony Express rider, galloped from the Pikes Peak Livery Stable two and a half blocks through the city and into the open doorway of the Pony Express office located in the imposing Patee House Hotel on the outskirts of town. After a lightning-fast dismount, the saddlebag-type mail pouch (later replaced by the *mochila*) containing letters and telegraph dispatches from the East, was ceremoniously placed across the saddle. He then stepped into the stirrup and straddled the bay mare. Seconds later, horse and rider bolted through the door and into history as the first westbound Pony Express rider. Historians have never fully agreed on whether it was Fry or Richardson who made that first epic ride. In either case it was the start of a legendary era in American history.

Three hours earlier, an enthusiastic crowd of merchants, bankers, riverboat crewmen, stage drivers, and gold seekers and settlers on their way west had gathered in the narrow streets of St. Joseph to witness the beginning of the "Greatest Enterprise of Modern Times."

An hour after the announced start time of 5 p.m., the mail from the East that was to be carried by the first westbound Pony rider had not yet arrived. All the speeches had been given, the band had played a number of stirring songs, and the bay mare that was to carry the westbound mail had been led to the town square and put on display to quiet the impatient crowds.

While the restless crowds were milling about the streets, Addison Clark, engineer for the Hannibal and St. Joseph Railroad, was steaming west from Hannibal to St. Joe with the special mail from the East that would be delivered by the Pony Express on its inaugural run west. Clark's train, the Missouri, was a single-engine locomotive pulling a tender, the special mail car, and a passenger car filled with dignitaries to attend the inaugural festivities. The messenger carrying the special mail from New York and Washington had missed his train connection from Detroit to Chicago, delaying his arrival in Hannibal by two hours. When the messenger finally arrived and the mail was safely aboard the Missouri, Clark blasted the horn and headed west, setting a speed record that, according to historians of the Pony Express, railroaders claimed stood for half a century.

When the Missouri finally pulled in to Hannibal, many of the spectators had returned to their farms or homes. But when Mayor Thompson called for three cheers for the Pony Express and three cheers for the first overland passage of the United States Mail, the remaining crowd gave a rousing cheer as the first westbound Pony Express rider galloped through the streets and onto the waiting paddle-wheel steamboat, which would cross the Missouri River into Kansas Territory, and begin his historic overland ride.

Nearly two thousand miles away, in San Francisco, enthusiastic crowds gathered to witness Pony Express rider James Randall leave the Alta Telegraph Office on Montgomery Street and head for the steamer *New World*, which would ferry him to Sacramento. There, a mail pouch would be passed to the first rider out of Sacramento, who would head east at 2:45 a.m. on April 4 to begin the first overland run east to St. Joseph. The first overland eastbound rider was Harry Roff, William Fisher, or William "Sam" Hamilton. Historians have never quite agreed on the identity of the first eastbound rider, either.

Where the West Began

In 1860 the busy town of St. Joseph, on the bend of the Missouri River, was where civilization ended and the sparsely inhabited West began. It was the logical choice as the eastern terminal of the Pony Express. It had railroad and telegraph lines connecting it to the cities in the East, and it was the largest town in that part of the Missouri River country. The St. Joseph city fathers, anticipating the glory, growth, and business this great adventure would bring their fair city, gave the company land, office space, and a host of other concessions to seal the deal with Russell, Majors, and Waddell to be the eastern terminal for the Pony Express.

Like many prominent cities in the Union, St. Joseph began as a fur-trading post. In 1826, five years after Missouri became a state, forty-three-year-old St. Louis–born fur trader Joseph Robidoux III, a crafty businessman with a visionary's eye on the future, convinced the American Fur Company that they needed a trading post at the foot of the Black Snake Hills on the bend of the Missouri River and that he should run it. For the next four years, Old Joe, as Robidoux was later known, traded goods, trinkets, tobacco, and frontier whiskey (watered-down alcohol) for furs brought to the post by Kickapoo, Iowa, Oto, Fox, and Potawatomi Indians. Then he quit the American Fur Company and worked as an independent, hiring as many as twenty men to trade with the Indians and making a tidy profit from the arrangement.

Old Joe was a man born to good luck. In 1834 he bought the Black Snake Hills Trading Post from the American Fur Company when European fashions changed from fur to silk and the fur business waned. Nine years later, in 1843, the great migration west along the Oregon Trail began. By then Old Joe had built a gristmill and launched a ferryboat to cross the Missouri River and two hundred people were living in the settlement around his trading post. That same year he filed plans with the Common Pleas in St. Louis to establish the town of Black Snake Hills. (In 1845 it would become known as St. Joseph, named after Robidoux's patron saint.) He promptly began selling lots for $100 to $150 to enterprising men who, like himself, envisioned the wealth that would be garnered from outfitting emigrants headed west. In 1848, five years after Old Joe established his town on the bend of the Missouri, gold was discovered in California and the "great migration west" turned into a stampede. Thousands of settlers arrived in St. Joseph by steamboat. Hundreds of wagon trains lined the streets, waiting to be ferried across the Missouri River. St. Joseph prospered, and Old Joe grew wealthy.

When the Pony Express was inaugurated in 1860, there were nearly nine thousand residents in St. Joseph and the town had all the amenities of a grand city: stables, stages, stores, saloons, hotels, and docks for the steamboats and ferries navigating the Missouri River. A year earlier the Hannibal and St. Joseph Railroad laid tracks

Patee House, built in 1858 by John Patee, served as a general office for the Pony Express in 1860. Courtesy Patee House Museum, St. Joseph, Missouri

Patee House, 150 years later. Bart Smith

across Missouri from Hannibal on the Mississippi River to St. Joseph on the Missouri River, bringing with it the telegraph line from the East. By 1859 St. Joseph, perched on the eastern edge of the western frontier, was linked by rail and wire to the seats of power in New York and Washington. A monument to its newfound status was the splendid four-story Patee House hotel, standing prominently on the outskirts of the city. Patee

House was equally as grand as the finest hotels in the East. Its luxurious accommodations served as the headquarters of the Pony Express, and the dignitaries of its parent company, the Central Overland California and Pikes Peak Express Company. (The official name of the company was a mouthful, so it was more often referred to as the Central Overland Company or COC.)

About two and half blocks west of Patee House stood the Pikes Peak Livery Stables where the Pony Express horses were housed. The stables were built in 1858 by Ben Holladay, later

Pikes Peak Livery Stables. The original stables built in 1858 housed approximately 200 horses. In the 1880s the St. Joseph Transfer Company remodeled the stables after they had been damaged by fire. The roof retained its original configuration and shingles; the walls were re-sided with brick. Courtesy Nebraska State Historical Society, Lincoln, Nebraska

This Pony Express Monument stands in Patee Park in St. Joseph across from the Pony Express Museum. The dedication ceremony for the monument took place on April 3, 1913. The ceremony included riders "Buffalo Bill" Cody, "Cyclone" Thompson and Charlie Cliff. The monument reads: "This monument erected by the Daughters of the American Revolution and the city of St. Joseph, marks the place where the first Pony Express rider started his run on April 3, 1860." Photograph courtesy The St. Joseph Museums, Inc., St. Joseph, Missouri

known as the "Stagecoach King." Holladay had amassed a fortune freighting and trading goods in New Mexico, Utah, and Colorado and investing in Nevada's Ophir Mine on the Comstock Lode. The well-heeled Holladay had been quietly loaning money to Russell, Majors, and Waddell to keep the debt-plagued Central Overland stage line and Pony Express operating. He held the deed to the Central Overland's properties as collateral for his loans and in 1862 acquired ownership of the company. Holladay parlayed that business into the greatest stagecoach empire in the West.

Thirty minutes after Fry or Richardson boarded the ferry, he was across the Missouri River at Elwood in Kansas Territory and headed for the relay station at Troy, making his way through five miles of thick forest. At Troy, he switched the mail pouch to a fresh horse and less than two minutes later was galloping across the prairie, changing mounts at Cold Springs, Kennekuk, Kickapoo, and Log Chain relay stations. Eight hours after his pony jumped off the ferry from St. Joseph, the Pony rider was seventy-seven miles west at the home station in Seneca and handing the mail to the next rider. Over the next 153 miles, the mail was passed on to three more riders, reaching Fort Kearny at 5:15 a.m. on April 5. Beyond Fort Kearny the relay riders followed the trail along the Platte River through the plains, passed Chimney Rock 535 miles out, rode through the Great Divide Basin along the Sweetwater River, passed the Wind River Range, and arrived in Salt Lake City on April 9, not quite six days after the mail left St. Joseph.

Night and day, relay after relay, the mail was rushed on through the wastelands of the Great Basin to the Mormon station in the foothills of the Sierra Nevada Mountains, where it was passed on to rider Warren Upson, who eight days earlier had carried the first eastbound mail through a blinding blizzard across the tortuous Sierra Nevada Mountains.

On the westbound run, Upson fared no better. The ten-foot-wide trail from Echo Summit to Lake Valley was covered with deep snow. Earlier that afternoon a large pack train had started down the mountain from the summit and was stuck in the snow halfway down. They couldn't go forward, and they couldn't go back. The owners of the train took the packs off the mules and left both the mules and the packs in the middle of the trail, then struggled through the snow back to the summit, where they made a fire and camped. Around midnight Upson came upon the mules and packs blocking the narrow trail. There was only one way to pass the mules without falling over the side of the mountain. He dismounted and broke a path for his horse around each mule. Three and half hours later, he had made his way around the mules and was on his way to Sportsman's Station in the valley of the Sacramento.

At Sportsman's station, rider William "Sam" Hamilton transferred the pouch to his saddled horse and galloped to Sacramento, reaching the city at 5:25 p.m. on April 13, 1860.

The mail from St. Joseph had reached Sacramento about two hours less than ten days. A cavalcade of citizens and fifteen of the Sacramento Hussars from Fort Sutter rode out to meet Hamilton and provide him a triumphal escort into the city. As he approached the city, a cannon salute fired, church and engine house bells rang out the news, and marching bands and cheering crowds turned out to greet Hamilton and celebrate the

ARRIVAL OF THE PONY EXPRESS AT SACRAMENTO, AND THE ENTHUSIASTIC RECEPTION BY THE INHABITANTS, 1860

An enthusiastic crowd of Sacramento citizens escort Pony rider "Sam" Hamilton and the first Pony Express mail into Sacramento. *New York Illustrated News,* May 19, 1860. Courtesy of California History Room, California State Library, Sacramento, California

successful inaugural run of the Pony Express. Meanwhile a telegrapher sent the news of Hamilton's arrival in Sacramento to San Francisco.

San Francisco in the 1850s was the most exciting city on Earth. It was a major seaport where ships from around the world anchored. Emigrants, sailors, and miners' gold from the Sierra Mountains kept the five hundred bars and one thousand gambling houses operating. Banks and brokerage houses lined Montgomery Street, and by the 1860s San Francisco had sprouted into one of the world's busiest financial centers. The

Alta Telegraph Office on the corner of Montgomery and Merchant Streets served as the western headquarters for the Pony Express. When the first mail from the east came in by Pony Express on April 14, 1860, at 12:38 a.m., a large assemblage of San Franciscans had gathered on the Broadway wharf to await the arrival of the steamer *Antelope.* As soon as the steamer came in sight, port fires were lit, rockets sent up, and a band played a martial air. When the steamer docked, the Pony Express rider and his horse, handsomely decorated for the occasion, came down the gangplank, where a procession of excited delegates followed them to the Pony Express headquarters.

About the time San Francisco started celebrating the arrival of the westbound mail, the

San Franciscans celebrate the arrival of the Pony Express with a torchlight procession. *New York Illustrated News,* May 19, 1860. Courtesy of California History Room, California State Library, Sacramento, California

eastbound Pony rider had reached St. Joseph, setting off another celebration in that city. Meanwhile two more Pony Express mail deliveries were already on their way.

"One by one the chains of darkness and desert are broken, and we are brought nearer and nearer to our brethren on the other side of the continent," lauded the April 13 *Daily Alta California* newspaper on the arrival of the mail from the east. The *San Francisco Daily Evening Bulletin* reminded readers that not only did the Pony Express connect California with our brethren on the other side of the continent, but with the world. The 1858 Ocean Telegraph cable from Ireland to Newfoundland connected the eastern United States with Europe and the Pony Express connected the American West to the eastern states and hence the world. "To be brought ten or twelve days nearer to the world is no small matter, nor one that will be without beneficial influence upon our prosperity."

History was made and legends born.

OVER PRAIRIE AND PLAIN

S t. Joseph was the jumping-off place for the westbound Pony riders and the headquarters for Pony Express Division One superintendent A. E. Lewis. We know little about Lewis other than he was an effective division manager. Like all division superintendents, he had the weighty task of overseeing the operations along his section of the trail: setting up home and relay stations and finding good men to operate them; seeing to it that the stations were regularly provisioned and had sound, fast horses waiting in the corrals; and hiring young riders willing to "risk death daily" to relay the mail across miles of often hostile country.

When one of Lewis's westbound Pony riders stationed in St. Joseph—Johnny Fry, Billy Richardson, Jack Keetley, or Charlie Cliff—jumped from the ferry that brought him across the Missouri River onto the frontier of the Great American West, the pounding hooves of his pony thundered through a thick forest of cottonwood, ash, oaks, elms, and hickory and onto the nearly treeless, grass-covered prairies of Kansas Territory. The path he rode was well worn—rutted by the wagon wheels of the pioneers and stagecoach travelers who headed west before him. He traveled over land that, nineteen years earlier in 1841, the pioneers making their way west over the Oregon Trail had described as an endless sea of tall grass billowing in a ceaseless, howling, nerve-racking wind. Small settlements dotted the prairie—the legacy of a few stout-hearted emigrants.

Bart Smith

*Sculpture of Pony Express
rider near Hanover, Kansas*

The emigrants who pulled out of the wagon trains to settle in this part of country in the 1840s stayed for many reasons—broken wagons, sickness, an unexplainable liking for the prairie lands. Many, perhaps most, stayed to profit from the emigrant traffic on the Oregon Trail and built "road ranches" near water if they could, dug deep wells, or hauled water long distances if necessary. The houses in this treeless country were usually built with sod and warmed with brush or buffalo chips (dried bison dung). Summer temperatures hovered at one hundred degrees or more for weeks on end, and winter temperatures dipped to forty below zero. They eked out a living selling food, supplies, wagon parts, and tools to emigrants headed to Oregon and California and to the Kansa, Otoe, Ottawa, Arapaho, and Kickapoo Indians that inhabited the area.

By the late 1850s small settlements sprang up around the road ranches. Many became stage stops serving Russell's L. & P. P. Express Co. from St. Joseph to California. By 1860, when the Pony

Dugout home in Nebraska. Nebraska State Historical Society, Lincoln, Nebraska

Express riders streaked through the small towns on the trail, the prairie was still virtually a sea of uninhabited rolling grasslands. It wasn't until after the Pony riders had made their last ride and the Civil War had ended that a surge of farmers from the east and immigrants from Europe began settling the grasslands and tried their hand at farming the obstinate land. These rugged pioneers of the prairies, more obstinate than the land they settled on, would later turn the grass prairies into some of the most productive farmland in the world.

Early Chroniclers of the Pony Express

During the time of the Pony Express, famed English explorer Sir Richard Burton rode the stage from St. Joseph, Missouri, to California and, as was his habit, kept a journal of his observations and later wrote *The Look of the West, 1860: Across the Plains to California* and *The City of the Saints and Across the Rocky Mountains to California*. Months after Burton's journey across the West, Samuel Clemens, who was not yet Mark Twain, took the stage to Virginia City. He titled his tale of crossing the West *Roughing It*. In writing of their adventures and describing the look of the West in 1860 and 1861, they quite accidentally penned much of what we know about the stations of the Pony Express. Fifty years would pass before the first book specifically about the Pony Express would be written. Newspaperman William Lightfoot Visscher, who endowed himself with the title of colonel, wrote *A Thrilling and Truthful History of the Pony Express with Other Sketches and Incidents of Those Stirring Times*. Some of what he wrote was doubtful, but he did indeed make it thrilling.

Above, Mark Twain. Library of Congress
Below, Sir Richard Francis Burton. Courtesy Print Collection, Miriam and Ira D. Wallach Division of Art, Prints and Photographs, The New York Public Library, Astor, Lenox and Tilden Foundations

Lost Stations

Although a good number of the Pony Express stations were built to profit from the emigrant traffic on the Oregon Trail, many others were built solely as relay stations for the Express mail. Towns grew up around the road ranches and stations and enjoyed a brisk business well past the period of the Pony Express. When the telegraph and railroads came through, bringing a close to the era of the overland stage and the Pony Express, many of the stations were converted to other purposes, and their remains still tell their story. Unfortunately, many were abandoned, were destroyed, or deteriorated and have turned to dust. These lost stations and their grand Old West beginnings are gone, and we mourn the loss.

Such is true of the first seven stations on the trail from St Joseph — Elwood, Troy, Cold Springs, Kennekuk, Kickapoo, Log Chain, and Seneca. The Elwood relay station, on the shores of the Missouri River in Kansas, was a stable where an eastbound rider stabled his tired horse if it was night and the ferry wasn't running. He then crawled into a waiting rowboat, and a man rowed him across the Missouri River to St. Joseph to deliver the eastbound mail. The westbound Express man, riding the horse he mounted in St. Joseph, rode his horse off the ferry and galloped straight through Elwood and on to Leonard Smith's stable adjacent to the Smith Hotel in Troy to change horses.

After a fast ride over the rolling hills from Troy, the rider pulled up to the crude cabin known as the Cold Springs stage station in what was then the small town of Syracuse. Cold Springs was also a stage stop manned by a woman and her four children, who tended the stock. The noted British explorer of Central and East Africa, Captain Sir Richard Francis Burton, traveled the American West in a Central Overland stage shortly after the Pony Express was inaugurated in 1860. In his detailed writings of the journey, he described the Cold Springs stage station as a "wretched log hut, which ignored the duster and the broom" and went on to describe the overpriced meal he was served for fifty cents as "a dinner consisting of donuts, green and poisonous with saleratus [baking soda], suspicious eggs in a massive greasy fritter, and rusty bacon, intolerably fat." While the condition of the log hut and the food was of vast importance to a weary traveler on an overland stage, it was of no importance to a Pony Express rider who stopped only long enough to change horses and never saw the inside of the "wretched hut" or tasted the "greasy fritters."

Johnny Fry, Romeo of the West

Pony Express riders were the heroes of their time, and Johnny Fry (often spelled Frey or Frye) was one of the most beloved of that proud band of history-making riders. He didn't make the longest or most dangerous ride. He is, however, credited by most historians and some newspapers of the day as the first Pony Express rider to leave St. Joseph on the inaugural run on April 3, 1860. Fry was a Kentucky farm boy who grew up in the saddle and could handle a horse. His family moved to Rushville, Missouri, in 1857 when he was seventeen. He gained local fame racing horses, and when he was twenty, he signed up to ride for the Pony Express. His regular run was between St. Joseph and Seneca.

Johnny Fry
The St. Joseph Museums, St. Joseph, Missouri

Young women adored Fry. They came out from their houses, shops, and farms to wave as he galloped past. One girl galloped her horse as close as she could get alongside Fry, grabbing at his red scarf. She missed but managed to tear off a piece of his shirttail, which she proudly sewed into a patchwork quilt. She was but one of his many admirers. Fry had a number of girlfriends along his route, and one of the tales of his adventures came from the town of Troy. As he galloped through the town, the Dooley sisters handed him pieces of cake to eat on his run. The handoff didn't always work well, and he dropped the cake. The Dooley sisters were determined that he should *have his cake. After some experiments they put holes in the center of the small cakes, which made it easier for Fry to hold on to them. This, according to the tale, was the birth of the American doughnut.*

People living along the trail are proud to claim they knew Fry or even that they saw him. To know or have seen the Pony Express rider somehow raised their social status. "I saw Johnny Fry many times. He was the first rider to ride west out of St. Joseph on the express," said Elizabeth Travelute during an interview with historian Florence Miller-Strauss and reported in Christopher Corbett's Orphans Preferred. "He was a nice young man. He wore a tight jacket, leggings and dark trousers. During the summer he wore a straw hat and in the winter a cap."

When the glory and fame of his time in the saddle as a Pony rider ended, the adventurous Fry enlisted in the Union Army, and many a heart was saddened when word came that he had been killed by Quantrill's Raiders at the Battle of Baxter Springs in Kansas.

Farther along the trail, the town of Kennekuk, named for a Kickapoo chief, was a growing settlement of one hundred people with two hotels, a livery, a blacksmith, wagon and harness shops, churches, and a post office. Tom Perry and his wife operated the Kennekuk stage and relay station. In contrast to the Cold Springs station, Mrs. Perry, the cook at the Kennekuk station, was acclaimed for her tasty food and good coffee. Pony riders no doubt inhaled a good whiff of sizzling bacon and fresh coffee as they changed horses and grabbed what the kindly Mrs. Perry handed them as they galloped full speed to the Kickapoo relay on the Kickapoo reservation (about twelve miles west of Horton, Kansas). The Kennekuk station disappeared with time, but in 1831 the Oregon Trail Memorial Association placed a Pony Express stone marker at its site.

The next change of horses was at the Log Chain relay and stage stop nestled in a grove of hickory and walnut trees. The large twenty-four-by-forty-foot log house and seventy-foot barn was built by Nobel H. Rising, who managed the Kickapoo station and whose son Dan was a Pony Express rider. There are two versions of why the station was named Log Chain. Some historians write that the name was a corruption of the name of the nearby creek known as Locknane. Others

Johnson William "Billy" Richardson

Billy Richardson was twenty-six when he took the Pony Express oath, and he too is believed by many historians to be the first Pony Express rider to leave St. Joseph on the run west to California. The St. Joseph Weekly West, dated April 7, 1860, reporting on the inaugural run of the Pony Express, credited Billy as the first rider. "The rider is a Mr. Richardson, formerly a sailor, and a man accustomed to every description of hardship, having sailed for years amid the snows and icebergs of the Northern Ocean."

Billy was born in 1834 in Virginia. According to an article written by his grand niece, Elaine Hartnagle, for History Buff, young Richardson was shanghaied and served on a seagoing freighter for several years before making a successful escape. The story of the first rider, as recalled by her grandmother and relayed by Elaine, is that the Pony riders drew straws to choose who would be the first rider. Fry won, but when the day of the ride came, he was not able to make the ride for reasons unknown, and Richardson was the first rider out of St. Joseph. We will never know whether Fry or Richardson made that first ride. Little else is known of Richardson except that he continued to ride for the Pony Express until it went out of business. He went to Fort Laramie (Wyoming) in Nebraska Territory, where his sister was teaching school. He died of pneumonia in Fort Laramie in 1862 at age twenty-eight.

claim frustrated pioneers and freighters who used log chains to pull their wagons out of the muddy-bottomed Locknane Creek hung the name on the station. Log Chain was extensively altered, but according to historians still stands on its original location and is listed on the Pony Express National Historic Trail.

The two-story Smith Hotel built in 1858 in Seneca was the first home station west of St. Joe and a welcome site to a Pony rider after riding seventy-seven miles over the plains. When he pulled up to the station, he handed the mail pouch to the next rider, who threw it over his saddle, jumped on his horse, and galloped away in a cloud of dust to the next relay.

The relay rider who headed west from Seneca made his first change of horses at the Ash Point relay managed by storekeeper John O'Laughlin. Burton, who passed through Ash Point in November 1860, noted that his stage stopped for water at "Uncle John's Grocery," where "Hang-dog Indians were seen squatting, standing and stalking about." The town of thirty people served as a stage stop in the 1860s, and by the end of the decade, it was a ghost town. What remains of the station is a stone-covered well dug by O'Laughlin and a 1930s marker with the text: "1858 Pony Express Station Overland Trail—Ash Point 240 Rods E."

Guittard's, a Favored Station of Travelers and Pony Riders

George Guittard arrived in Kansas in 1857 and built the earliest permanent settlement in that part of Kansas. Burton described Guittard's as a "clump of board houses on the far side of a shady, well-wooded creek—the Vermillion, a tributary of the Big Blue River, so called from its red sandstone bottom, dotted with granitic[sic] and porphyritic boulders." He went on to describe the station house as "clean, the fences neat; the ham and eggs, the hot rolls and coffee fresh and good." Guittard's son, Xavier, managed the station, which alternated as a home or relay station as well as a stage stop. A large, two-story house provided living quarters and a waiting room for stage passengers, and the barn had a blacksmith shop and stalls for twenty-four horses. The house was dismantled in 1910, and the lumber was used to build a new house on the same site. Not all of the old Guittard station was lost. A door salvaged from the original station was hung in a second-story room. A stone marker, with a bronze plaque from the Oregon Trail Memorial Association, was placed near the site in June 1931. The text on the marker reads: "1860-61 Guittard Station—East 80 Rods Oregon Trail."

Bunks for the Pony Express riders. Bart Smith

When the rider left Guittard's, the route took him to the Big Blue River country and the stone Pony Express station in the prospering town of Marysville on the banks of the Big Blue River. Erstwhile traveler Sir Richard Burton described Marysville as a town that thrived "by selling whiskey to ruffians of all descriptions." Elizabeth Mohrbacher Travelute, who came to Marysville in a caravan of prairie schooners when she was fourteen, described the country between Guittard's and Marysville during the days of the Pony Express, explaining that there was "not a log cabin or a dugout between this city and the Vermillion Creek. It was all a vast plain, no laid-out roads, no cattle grazing in green pastures, and the only human beings who might cross your path was a squad of Otoe Indians, who were out on a hunt for a living. A pack of prairie wolves would frequently be seen and their desperate howling would fill the lonesome traveler with fright." She went on to reminisce about the days of the Pony Express:

Marshall Ferry. After leaving Marysville, the rider normally forded the Big Blue River, but when the river was flooding Robert Shibley operated Frank Marshall's rope-drawn ferry, like this one, to carry Pony Express riders and horses across. Bart Smith

"I can still remember hearing and seeing the riders come galloping down from Schmidt's pasture at the east edge of what was then the town. Just before they came in sight at the top of the hill they blew a horn. It was a shiny tin horn and the rider

Left, vegetable garden behind the Hollenberg Station.
Bart Smith

Below, the Hollenberg Pony Express Station in Hanover, Kansas, is the only original unaltered Pony Express station still standing. In 1941 the Kansas State Legislature purchased the station and the surrounding acreage to preserve the site. The Kansas State Historical Society manages the site, and it is listed as a National Historic Landmark. Kansas State Historical Society

carried it in the back of his saddle bag. When he blew the horn it was a signal to Jacob Weisbach, my brother-in-law, who was the postmaster, to have the mail ready. He had to be out of the post office with the mail in his hands so he could give it to the riders."

Two Marysville businessmen, Joseph H. Cottrell and Hank Williams, had contracted with Russell, Majors, and Waddell in 1859 to build and lease a stone livery stable to the Pony Express for a relay station. A blacksmith's shop was on one end of the stable and stalls on the other. Apparently there were times when the Marysville relay was used as a home station. In that case the riders stayed at the American Hotel, north of the livery. The livery stable was later converted to a garage, produce station, and cold storage lock plant. The board roof of the stable burned in 1876, and a hip-style roof was added to the building. In 1931 a marker was placed at the Marshall County Courthouse identifying Marysville as a home station of the Pony Express.

Hollenberg, the Last Station in Kansas

After crossing the Big Blue River and the cross-roads of the St. Joseph and Independence Roads, the rider pulled up at the Hollenberg station in the Little Blue River Valley. Its proprietor, German-born G. H. Hollenberg, came to Kansas Territory in 1857 and built the hotel and stage stop. It was the first real building for miles around and considered one of the best stage stations in a hundred miles. By 1860, when the station became a stop for Pony Express riders, Hollenberg already had a booming business selling goods, livestock, and feed to emigrants headed to Oregon, California, and Utah. Joseph Dicerto noted in *Saga of the Pony Express* that a dozen people could be quartered on the second floor of the hotel, and at times more than a hundred travelers were camped on the grounds. Hollenberg's place also had a huge barn that could stable as many as a hundred horses and made a good home station for the Pony Express riders. The barn's loft, which ran the entire length of the building, was turned into sleeping quarters for the station keepers and riders, and meals were served at the hotel.

On to the Nebraska Plains

Beyond the Big Blue crossing and Hollenberg's home station, the trail followed the Little Blue River north into Nebraska to the Platte River. It was still very much a barren wilderness except for the stage and Pony Express stations along the

Shootout at Rock Creek

James Butler Hickok.
Adams Museum and House, Inc., Deadwood,
South Dakota

James Butler Hickok, later to be known as "Wild Bill" and to become famous as a gunslinger, gambler, lawman, and western hero in Buffalo Bill's Wild West Show, was born in Illinois in 1837. At eighteen he fled to Kansas in the mistaken belief that he had killed a man. Hickok was working as a stock tender at the Rock Creek relay when, on the hot afternoon of July 12, 1861, the "McCanles Gang" rode in and a Wild West legend was born.

In Hickok's version of the gunfight, as told in Harper's magazine in 1867, McCanles was the leader of a gang of ten desperadoes, horse thieves, murderers, and cutthroats who were the terror of everybody on the border and, worse yet, were Southern sympathizers. He went on to tell a hair-raising, bloodthirsty tale of how he dispatched McCanles and his gang that thrilled easterners and added to Hickok's popularity as a western gunman.

Hickok is known to have been the biggest bald-faced liar of the western lawmen. His stories of his own exploits knew no boundaries of reason or possibility. He once claimed he picked off fifty Confederate soldiers with fifty bullets and a wonder-working rifle. Thus Hickok's story of what happened at Rock Creek is taken with a grain of salt by most historians.

What is believed to have happened is that David McCanles, his son William, his cousin James Woods, and a hired hand named James Gordon rode to Rock Creek to collect money they were owed by the owners of the Pony Express. McCanles confronted Horace

Wellman, the station keeper, insisting on his money, which Wellman claimed he didn't have. Wellman went into the house, possibly to get a gun, while his feisty common-law wife, Jane Holmes, loudly argued with McCanles. No one recalled what happened next, but the shooting started. McCanles was shot dead either by Hickok coming from the stables toward the station or Wellman from inside the house. Then Hickok and Wellman killed Gordon and Woods. Twelve-year-old William escaped unharmed.

Adding intrigue to the story of Hickok and McCanles is that, according to Charles Dawson in his 1912 book *Pioneer Tales of the Oregon Trail and of Jefferson County*, twenty-year-old Kate Shell, who lived on the west side of Rock Creek, was McCanles's mistress who had followed him from North Carolina. While at Rock Creek, Kate had also captured the affections of Hickok, and the situation didn't set well with either man.

Hickok and Wellman were charged with murder and both were acquitted. Hickok left the Rock Creek station unscathed by the event and joined the Union Army as a scout.

In fairness to Hickok, some of his deeds were real. In 1868, while again serving as an army scout in Colorado, Hickok galloped through attacking Indians to get help and saved thirty-four men. Later he was appointed sheriff in Hays City and Abilene, Kansas, and said to have killed four men in the line of duty. He was described in Paul Trachtman's *The Gunfighters* as an awesome figure in those towns "with his back to the wall, looking at everything and everybody from under his eyebrows—just like a mad bull." In 1871 the Abilene city council fired him for loosening a barrage of gunfire at a group of drunks, killing one of the drunks and one law officer. By 1872 Hickok was appearing on stage with "Buffalo Bill" Cody and a host of other notorious gunfighters of the Wild West.

Hickok went to Dakota Territory in 1876 and was shot from behind by a saddle tramp while playing poker in a Deadwood saloon. He held what has since been known as the dead man's hand—aces and eights.

Stable where Hickok wrangled horses for the Pony Express, Rock Creek Historic Park, Nebraska. Bart Smith

trail. A scattering of wooden crosses told of hard times on the Nebraska plains, where countless numbers of pioneers died, usually from disease or accidents, trying to make their way west during the great migration.

The rider heading west from Hollenberg's made his first change of horses at the isolated Rockhouse relay and then galloped on to the Rock Creek station, which was soon to become famous in western lore as the site of the McCanles-Hickok gunfight.

The original Rock Creek station began as a road ranch on the Oregon Trail. The small cabin, barn, and lean-to that was set up to store and sell hay, grain, and supplies to travelers along the trail was built on the west side of Rock Creek. It was subsequently used as an Overland stage stop.

David McCanles left North Carolina for the goldfields of Colorado in 1859. Seeing the long line of disappointed gold seekers, he went on to Nebraska with the high hopes of making money off struggling pioneers headed to California. He settled at Rock Creek near the old Oregon Trail road ranch. McCanles built a toll bridge across Rock Creek and on the east side of the creek built a sixteen-by-thirty-six-foot-long rough-hewn log cabin with an attic accessible from the outside and an impressive stone fireplace. The following year McCanles leased the east-side property to the Pony Express as a relay station. A. E. Lewis hired Horace Wellman and his common-law wife, Jane Holmes, as station keepers and James W. "Dock" Brink and James Butler Hickok as stock tenders.

"A weary drive over a rough and dusty road, through chill night air and clouds of mosquitoes, which we were warned would accompany us to the Pacific slope of the Rocky Mountains, placed us about 10 p.m. at Rock, also called Turkey Creek—surely a misnomer, no turkey ever haunted so villainous a spot!" wrote Sir Richard Burton, who went on to add that "the ranch was a nice place for invalids, especially for those of the opposite sex. Upon the bedded floor of the foul 'doggery' lay, in a seemingly promiscuous heap, men, women, children, lambs and puppies all fast in the arms of Morpheus, and many under the influence of a much jollier god. The employees, when aroused pretty roughly, blinked their eyes in the atmosphere of smoke and mosquitoes and declared that it had been 'merry in the hall' that night—the effects of which merriment had not passed off. About half an hour's dispute about who should do the work, they produced cold scraps of mutton and a kind of bread which deserves a totally distinct generic name. The strongest stomachs of the party made tea, and found some milk which was not more than one quarter flies. This succulent meal was followed by the usual douceur. On this road, however mean or wretched the fare, the station-keeper, who is established by the proprietor of the line, never derogates by lowering his price."

Today the site is part of the Rock Creek Station State Historical Park, three miles northeast of Endicott, Nebraska. An Oregon Trail and Pony Express marker lies near the park entrance. Reconstructed station buildings by the Nebraska Game and Parks Commission also stand within the park.

The Longest Ride

British-born Jack Keetley was eighteen when he was hired by A. E. Lewis to make the express run from Marysville to Big Sandy. On one run Jack's relief riders were not available for unknown reasons, and he carried the eastbound mail from Big Sandy to Elwood, exchanged mail pouches with a man waiting to take it across the river to St. Joseph, and then carried the westbound mail back to Seneca. He rode the 340 miles in thirty-one hours without rest, eating as he rode. In the last five miles to Seneca, he fell asleep. As Keetley slipped from the saddle at Seneca, the next rider grabbed the mochila and headed west. The mail never stopped moving, and Keetley had earned his place of honor among Pony Express riders.

When the Pony Express disbanded in 1861, Keetley went mining in Utah. Adapting to mining as easily and as conscientiously as he did the Pony Express, he eventually became superintendent of the Little Bell and King mines near Park City, Utah. He worked in mining until he was sixty-five and died in Salt Lake City six years later in 1912.

Richard Egan, a rider in Division Four, nearly equaled Keetley's ride. Egan logged 330 miles in the saddle to oblige another rider who wanted to take off to visit his sweetheart.

Jack Keetley rode 340 miles to take the mail through and is honored among Pony Express riders as making the longest ride. The St. Joseph Museums, Inc., St. Joseph, Missouri

Rock Creek relay was famous for its gunfights, mosquitoes, and late-night merriment, but a fast-traveling Pony Express rider had little opportunity to enjoy the titillating stories during his quick change of horses before he was off to the relay at Virginia City and the home station at Big Sandy, where quite possibly he would hear the news of what happened up and down the trail.

As the relief rider left Big Sandy, he galloped over the Nebraska plains to the Thompson and Kiowa relays, then six more miles to the dreaded Narrows. Here the land abruptly changed from prairie to low, steep bluffs and the trail became a narrow strip of land along the banks of the Little Blue River. Just beyond the Narrows, the Little Blue and Liberty Farm relays and stage stops waited for the hoof beats of the approaching Pony Express horses. They came and went with a fast change of horses, and the westbound rider galloped on to the Thirty-Two Mile station. This long, one-story station was thirty-two miles from Fort Kearny. Once the rider left the Thirty-Two Mile station, he had two more changes of horses, one at Sand Hill and the next at Hooks. In a series of raids on stations and road ranches, Cheyenne and Sioux warriors burned the Liberty Farm, Lone Tree, and Thirty-Two Mile stations during the Indian War of 1864.

Fort Kearny on the Platte

In the 1840s the United States War Department decided to establish a chain of military posts across the West to protect the flood of emigrants and travelers crossing the unsettled territories of the western frontier on their way to Oregon. In 1846 the army built its first post along the Missouri River at the mouth of Table Creek. Camp Kearny was named to honor Colonel Stephen W. Kearny, who located the site. The army soon realized that its location on the Missouri was too far from the Oregon Trail to be of value to the stream of emigrants headed west. In 1847 the army sent Lieutenant Daniel P. Woodbury to select a site along the Platte River. "I have located the post opposite a group of wooded islands in the Platte River . . . three miles from the head of the group of islands called Grand Island." In the spring of 1848, Camp Kearny at Table Creek was abandoned and all the men were marched to the head of Grand Island to build the first military station on the trail to Oregon—Fort Kearny. It became a vital trail stop for emigrants. The fort housed large stores of goods, and the commander of the fort was authorized to sell at cost or, if the situation warranted it, to give supplies to emigrants.

Interior of Fort Kearny blacksmith shop. Bart Smith

By June 1849, Woodbury noted in his journals that four thousand wagons had passed the fort so far that year. Most were "49ers" on their way to "strike it rich" in California. By 1860, when the Pony Express was established, Fort Kearny was a busy freight, stage, and mail stop. It hummed with the plodding footfalls of oxen, mules, and horses; the creak of freight wagons, prairie schooners, and

Conestoga wagons; and the pounding hoof beats of mounted army patrols and Pony Express riders coming and going. During the violent summer of 1864, when the Cheyenne and Sioux—angry over the never-ceasing encroachment into their lands—raided wagon trains, stages, and road ranches along the Platte and Little Blue Rivers, the soldiers from Fort Kearny gave refuge to fleeing settlers at the fort and escorted wagon trains across the plains.

Fort Kearny State Historical Park, Kearney, Nebraska. Bart Smith

When the tracks of the Union Pacific Railroad crossed Nebraska, Fort Kearny was no longer needed and was abandoned in 1871. Four years later the buildings were torn down and the materials moved to North Platte and Sidney. In 1876 the grounds were transferred to the Department of the Interior to be turned over to homesteaders. In 1928, fifty-seven years after the fort was abandoned, the citizens of Nebraska formed the Fort Kearny Memorial Association to raise money to purchase and restore the grounds. Forty acres of the original site were acquired and turned over to the State of Nebraska in 1929. It is now operated as Fort Kearny State Historical Park and listed on the National Register of Historic Places.

Fort Kearny played an important role in the settlement of the West and in the operation of the Pony Express. Because it was a military post, there is some doubt that it was an official Pony Express station. Pony Express riders brought in and carried out military dispatches and mail from Fort Kearny, and there is no doubt they were frequently in the fort. Whether it was a station where they changed horses and riders is a question that has never been convincingly answered. Two miles west of Fort Kearny was a small settlement known as Doby Town, which may have been the Pony Express station.

Fort Kearny was the last station in Lewis's Division One. The relay rider west from Fort Kearny rode in superintendent Jack Slade's Division Two.

5

ALONG THE PLATTE

Pony Express Division Two, under the watchful eye of its superintendent gunman Jack Slade, began west of Fort Kearny at the Platte station in the plains and valleys of the Platte River and ended at Horseshoe, Wyoming.

The Platte River lazily winds its way across the prairies and plains from the Rocky Mountains to the Missouri River and has been described by early travelers as "a mile wide and an inch deep" and "bad to ford, destitute of fish, too dirty to bathe in and too thick to drink." The land on both sides of the river was flat and treeless and gradually rose in sandstone cliffs. Acres and acres of prairie dog villages inhabited the Platte River Valley, and antelope and buffalo grazed the short grasses along with their predator enemies—black bears, grizzlies, coyotes, and wolves. Riders of the Pony Express Trail heading west from the Platte station followed the river along its south bank to the confluence of the North and South Platte Rivers near today's city of North Platte, Nebraska. Then in a southwestward trek they galloped along the south fork of the river to South Platte, Julesburg, and Overland City in Colorado. At Overland the trail turned abruptly northward and climbed in a difficult overland journey to again follow the North Platte River through Nebraska and Wyoming.

Bart Smith

North Platte with
Distant Scotts Bluff.

Jack Slade—Desperado of the Rockies

The Pony Express had its share of colorful characters, including stock tender "Wild Bill" Hickok and Pony rider William "Buffalo Bill" Cody, but none was more feared than Division Two superintendent Slade.

"From Fort Kearny, west, he was feared a great deal more than the Almighty," quoted Mark Twain in *Roughing It*. He went on to write that Slade was "an efficient servant of the Overland (stage and Pony Express), an outlaw among outlaws and yet their relentless scourge."

Joseph Alfred "Jack" Slade, the son of Congressman Charles Slade, was born in Carlyle, Illinois, in 1821, 1828, or perhaps 1831 (historians have never been able to nail this down). His path to becoming the infamous Jack Slade started at age thirteen, when he killed a man by hitting him in the head with a rock. Some sources say that the man was bothering Slade and his friends, and Slade threw the rock to put a stop to it. Whatever the cause or anticipated consequence, Slade skedaddled to Texas to hide from the law. In 1847 he served as an army trooper in the war with Mexico.

During the 1850s Slade captained trains of freight wagons, then turned to driving a stagecoach. In 1859 he was hired by Russell, Majors, and Waddell's general superintendent, Benjamin F. Ficklin, to supervise their Central Overland California and Pikes Peak Company stage and mail service operations in the stretches of Nebraska, Colorado, and Wyoming, where thieves were "congregated along the route and were systematically preying upon the company's property," attacking the coaches and stealing the stock. Adding to the crooked mix were some stage station employees who were secretly snatching supplies and cash. Slade treated any wrongdoing in his division as a personal affront and relentlessly wrought his own form of justice on the perpetrator. Whether truth or lore, early newspapers and storytellers reported that while Slade was in charge of operations, crooked stage station employees were dispatched one way or another—fired, killed, or wisely took off for parts unknown—and horse stealing and stage holdups were rare. "True," wrote Mark Twain, "in order to bring about this wholesome change Slade had to kill several men—some say three—but, others say four and others say six—but the world was the richer for their loss."

Slade, working from his headquarters in Horseshoe, supervised the operations in Division Two until the Pony Express was halted and Ben Holladay took over Russell, Majors, and Waddell's Central Overland stage line. Holladay hired Slade

An Abundance of Prairie Dogs

Young Howard Ransom Egan, who later became a Pony Express rider, was traveling with his father during the 1848 Mormon migration to Salt Lake and recalled, "The whole earth seemed to be covered with little mounds. . . . We could see dozens of the dogs at a time sitting upright and watching our train, and if a person started towards them there would be a general barking chorus and instantly every dog would disappear and not appear again till the intruder had left to a safe distance."

—Excerpted from William G. Hartley's Howard Egan's 1848 Trek in the Mormon Historical Studies.

Engraving of a prairie dog town in Nebraska. Nebraska State Historical Society, Library/ Archives Division, Lincoln, Nebraska

to continue overseeing stage operations in that dangerous and bandit-ridden stretch of country.

Slade's reputation and success in quelling thefts and stage holdups in his division earned him the gratitude of his employer, but eventually his temper, hard drinking, and frequent drunken thrashings of innocent patrons in local saloons forced Holladay to fire him. Slade drifted toward Virginia City, Montana, where in March 1864 his hell-raising drunkenness and gun-brandishing threats got him hanged by Montana vigilantes.

Slade's Division Two westward bound Pony riders traveled along the sandy banks of the North Platte in a slight uphill grade, changing horses at Garden, Plum Creek, and Willow Island relays and finally reaching the home station at Midway. The Plum Creek relay was both a stage stop and Pony Express relay and later a telegraph station. In the Indian wars of 1864, a small garrison of troops was stationed there. The Garden station was burned in 1865 and Plum Creek was burned in 1867, but a small cemetery near the station contains the graves of victims of the Indian attacks. The Willow Island relay was moved to Cozad's Park for Boy Scout gatherings. A 1938 plaque identifies it as a Pony Express station.

Pony rider Richard Cleve, who rode between the Platte and Midway stations, recollected that the winters in Nebraska were more dangerous to the Pony riders than the Indians. He left the Midway station and headed east in "one of the worst blizzards that I ever saw, and I have seen a good many of them for I was in western Nebraska for nine years." He rode all day through the howling winds and snow, arriving at the Platte home station late that night. His relief rider was sick, so he went on toward the Thirty-Two Mile station. Seven miles out he found the snow so deep and the blizzard so blinding it was impossible to find the road. "I tried it several times, but gave it up, so I dismounted and led the horse back and forth until day light." He finally made his way to the station, recalling that "I got to the station about nine o'clock, hungry as a wolf. It was forty below zero." But there was no relief rider at the station. He ate some breakfast, climbed on a fresh horse, and headed to Liberty Farm, the next station east. There was no relief rider there or at the Kiowa station twenty-eight miles farther. "That twenty-eight miles tired me more than all the others. There was twenty or more deep gullys that were drifted full of snow. I had to dismount, lead the horse and kick and tramp the snow to get the horse through. I got there about dark and no rider from the east yet." Cleve rode on to Big Sandy, where a stock tender offered to take his place. He had been in

Above, the Midway Pony Express Station on the Williams Ranch in the Platte Valley, ca. 1896. Courtesy Nebraska State Historical Society

Left, the Willows Island station was moved from its site near Lexington to Cozad, Nebraska. Bart Smith

Right, nearly 150 years later the Midway station is none too worse for the wear, as shown in this 2006 photograph. Bart Smith

the saddle for thirty-six hours riding 160 miles in near forty below weather. "I went to the house as soon as the young man started with the mail. I saw a cot in the corner of the room and went for it. I believe I was asleep before I even got to it."

West of the Midway station, the Pony rider changed horses four times—at Gilman's, Matchette's, Cottonwood, and Cold Springs—before coming into the home station at Freemont Springs.

The relief rider from Freemont Springs made his first stop at O'Fallon's Bluff, where a sign told travelers they were now four hundred miles west of St. Joseph, Missouri. To weary travelers who had already come so far, it may have been comforting news to know they had managed to make it that far. But for those determined to make it to the West Coast, it was a painful reminder that, depending on their destination, they still had fifteen hundred or more rocking, rolling, back-jolting wagon or stage miles to go, depending on their destination. For the Pony Express rider in this stretch of trail, it was two more changes of horses at Alkali and Sand Hill before he reached his home station at Diamond Springs and turned the mail over to the next rider.

Cottonwood Pony Express Station in Nebraska. Nebraska State Historical Society

The Killing of Jules Beni

One victim of Jack Slade's deadly revenge on thieves who had the audacity to steal, cheat, or otherwise cause problems in his division of authority was Jules Beni (historians have also spelled his name as Bernard, Reni, and Rene). He had set up a trading post near Lodgepole Creek to trade with the Cheyenne Indians and later the emigrants heading west. He founded the rough and ready town of Julesburg that grew up around the post in what is now Colorado. In 1859 the Central Overland California and Pikes Peak Express Company leased or bought the trading post to be used as a stagecoach way station. Beni was kept on as stationmaster. He was a shrewd, dangerous man of considerable notoriety. As related in *Wyoming Tales and Trails*, Eugene Ware, an army captain serving in the area, wrote: "He had killed several persons, and had become a great deal of a character in the country. A man who had known him several years told me that Jules once killed two persons of local celebrity, cut off their ears, dried them, and carried these four ears in his pockets. That every once in a while he would take them out and show them to somebody. They were great trophies, as he thought."

There are many versions of what happened, but the story goes that in the stretch of country where Beni had his ranch and operated the Julesburg station, robberies and horse stealing were rampant. Some newspapers of the times reported that Beni was the "cutthroat" leader of a gang of bandits and horse thieves profiting from the stage and express traffic on the trail. When the Central Overland California and Pikes Peak Express Company's general superintendent, Benjamin Ficklin, heard what was going on, he told Jack Slade to fire Beni. Slade wasted no time in telling Beni to clear out and replacing him with George Chrisman. It was sometime after the era of the Pony Express and while Slade was working for Ben Holladay's Overland stage line along the same route that the bitter and still angry Beni

Jack Slade blasts away at the slumped body of Jules Beni in this sketch by Charles Russell. Drawing by Charles M. Russell, ca. 1922, ink and graphite on paper, 14 x 22 inches. Courtesy Amon Carter Museum, Fort Worth, Texas

ambushed Slade, wounding him with a shot to the stomach. When Slade recovered, he sent some of his men to hunt down Beni.

Slade had Beni lashed to a corral post (one source said a dry-goods box), then used him for target practice. The grim scene lasted until twenty-two bullets were fired into the dying and then dead Beni. In Slade's final act of revenge, and in a bit of grim irony, he cut off Beni's ears, nailed one to the station door, and used the other to make a watch fob that he proudly carried—or so the story goes.

Crossing the South Platte

What the O'Fallon's Bluff sign didn't tell travelers, but that the Pony riders knew, was that from O'Fallon's, the place where the Oregon Trail crossed the South Platte River was less than sixty miles away. This well-known crossing was named by early emigrants as the Fort Laramie Crossing, Ash Hollow Crossing, and Brule Crossing. Following the 1849 gold rush, it became known as the California Crossing. The Overland stage and Pony Express Trail crossed the South Platte about twelve to fifteen miles upriver from the California Trail crossing. This upriver crossing also became known as the California Crossing and the old crossing as the Lower California Crossing.

When stage travelers and Pony Express riders came ashore on the other side of the California Crossing, they were at Julesburg—the "toughest town west of the Missouri River." Julesburg was a stomping ground for loose women, gamblers, and crooks, where saloons served the "vilest of liquor at two bits a glass," and the hangout of horse thieves and desperadoes who preyed on travelers. While the trail from and to Julesburg was a risky run for stage passengers and the U.S. mail carried by stage, there were no recorded incidents of attacks on Pony Express riders by Julesburg toughs. Holladay changed the name of the town to Overland City in a vain attempt to change its image. Although the town

Emigrants crossing the South Platte River at "California Crossing."
Painting by W. H. Jackson. Courtesy Scotts Bluff National Monument, Nebraska

Mud Springs Station Monument. Bart Smith

was moved several times over the years, it kept its Julesburg name.

Beyond Julesburg the trail climbed upward, heading northwesterly to connect with the Oregon Trail along the North Platte River. The Pony rider changed horses at Lodge Pole and again at Pole Creek station two. Then twice more, first at Pole Creek station three—where the relay station was a dugout in the side of a hill with a board front and a couple of boxes for chairs, a

Left, this 400-foot-high pile of clay and volcanic ash was dubbed the Court House by pioneers for its resemblance to a municipal building in St. Louis. A Pony Express station by the same name was along the trail near the rock. Bart Smith

Below, fourteen miles west of Courthouse Rock stood the dramatic 500-foot-tall stone spire named by pioneers as Chimney Rock. After noting the mound of debris at the base of this magnificent oddity, early pioneers realized that it was slowly eroding from wind and water. Today the spire is 325 feet tall. Bart Smith

tin washbasin, a water pail, and a single towel for public use—and then at the second Midway Station in this division, of which little is known. Less than an hour later, he pulled up to the sod shack of the Mud Springs home station and turned the mail pouch over to the relief rider.

The Pony Express relief rider headed west from the Mud Springs station, galloping over a stretch of trail that traversed country that was barren and eerily awesome. It was marked by monuments of ancient natural upheavals—Courthouse Rock, Chimney Rock, Scott's Bluff, and the abandoned wagons and graves of emigrants plodding toward Salt Lake City, Oregon, and California.

After a quick change of horses at the Chimney Rock station, the Pony rider hightailed it to Ficklin's station, switched mounts, and rode through Mitchell Pass to the home station at Scott's Bluff on the bend of the North Platte River. Then relay by relay, the mail was rushed on to Fort Laramie.

The Many Faces of Fort Laramie

Laramie Peak, Fort Laramie, and the nearby Laramie River were named for French-Canadian trapper Jacques LaRamee. LeRamee was a leader of "free trappers" who trapped the waters of the North Platte around 1818 and had arranged the first trappers' rendezvous in Wyoming. LeRamee set up his trapper's camp at the fork of the Platte that would become known as La Ramie's River, Laremais', and Laramie's Fork. LeRamee was killed in 1819 by Arapahos. Some reports say that LaRamee was found facedown in the river, and others claim LaRamee's partners found him and buried him where he lay.

In late May 1834, William Sublette and Robert Campbell camped there on their way to the rendezvous at Ham's Fork on the Green River. Sublette apparently decided then and there to build a trader's fort at the mouth of Laramie's Fork and the North Platte River. The foundation was laid on June 1 and the trading post christened Fort William. A year later Sublette and Campbell sold Fort William to mountain man Jim Bridger and his partners. Bridger and company turned it over to the American Fur Company. Sublette's Fort William was referred to as "Fort la Ramee" by Father DeSmet while making his 1840 journey through this part of the country to bring Christianity to the Indians.

By the spring of 1841, Lancaster P. Lupton, a competitive trader from the South Platte River, built an adobe-walled Fort Platte nearby. In a fur- trader's game of one-upmanship, Pierre Chouteau Jr. and Company, who then owned

Old Fort Laramie. Painting by W. H. Jackson. Courtesy Scotts Bluff National Monument

the former American Fur Company and Fort William, built a new adobe fort of its own on the banks of the Laramie. The new adobe trading post was named Fort John, but despite its official name was known on the frontier as Fort Laramie.

The growing number of emigrants traveling the Oregon Trail and the increasing unrest among

Sutler's Store at Fort Laramie. Prior to the Civil War, civilians operating the army post supply store were known as sutlers. After the war they were given the title of "post trader." National Park Service, Fort Laramie National Historic Site, Fort Laramie, Wyoming

the Indians opposing mass encroachments into their territory prompted President James Polk in 1846 to sign "an act to provide for raising a regiment of Mounted Riflemen and for military stations on the route to Oregon." The first such post was Fort Kearny on the Lower Platte River, and the second to be constructed was "near Fort Laramie, a trading station belonging to the American Fur Company." The directive further authorized the Corps of Engineers to purchase the buildings of Fort Laramie if it was deemed necessary to do so.

In June 1849 the fur-trading post of Fort William known as Fort Laramie was sold to the United States to be used as a temporary military post, and by July a small garrison of troops had arrived. At the end of the month, Colonel Aeneas Mackay, who had been sent to inspect the post, reported to Quartermaster General Thomas Jesup that "it is a good deal in decay and needs repairs. Those, the Engineers are employed in making and in addition have commenced the construction of quarters outside the walls. . . ." The

Foundation of all that remains of troop barracks at Fort Laramie. Bart Smith

annual report for 1849 reflected the chief engineer's optimistic assessment of their progress: "The building now under way, and which are expected to be ready for use before winter, are, a two-story block of officer's quarters, containing 16 rooms; a block of soldiers' quarters, intended for one company, but which will be occupied by two during the coming winter; a permanent bakery, and two stables for one company each. . . ."

Materials from the old adobe fort were used in construction of the new Fort Laramie. By 1870 the last remnants of the old fort had disappeared and officer's quarters were built on the site. In 1890 Fort Laramie was abandoned and local ranchers desperate for building materials dismantled most of the buildings. A few buildings remain — the brick-lined two-story block of officers' quarters and the adobe section of the sutler's store building where frontier travelers could get supplies for their journey. Fort Laramie was designated a National Monument in 1938 and a National Historic Site in 1960.

The End of the High Plains

Fort Laramie marked the end of the High Plains and the beginning of the long ascent into the rugged Rocky Mountains. The uphill run from east to west drained the energy of the ponies, and relays were spaced closer together, some only eight to ten miles apart. Nine miles from Fort Laramie, the rider galloped into the Sand Point station (also known as Nine Mile station and Ward station) in the shadow of Register Cliff, where the thousands of emigrants that had passed this way before inscribed their stories in the one-hundred-foot-high sandstone precipice. With a fresh mount beneath him, the rider urged his pony through the ridge of soft sandstone ruts worn by their wagons wheels. A little farther on he came into the Cottonwood Station and then rode on to the home station at Horseshoe Creek. The Horseshoe station was the last station west in Division Two on the Pony Express Trail. It was Jack Slade's headquarters.

In the town of Guernsey, Wyoming, an Oregon Trail marker identifies the site of the Horseshoe Creek station as 530 yards south of Highway 26 at the edge of a park.

Bart Smith

View of the Sweetwater River through a gap near the site of the Three Crossings Pony Express Station.

6

ALONG THE SWEETWATER RIVER
TO THE SALT LAKE VALLEY

The Division Three superintendent was James Erwen Bromley, who knew the country, had experience ramrodding a stage and mail business, and knew a good horse when he saw one. He was a splendid horseman who openly enjoyed a good horse race and picked the best and fastest mustangs he could find for the Pony Express.

Like many young men who itched to go west, the former Illinois and Missouri stage driver and line superintendent had made his way across the plains and mountains of the Kansas and Nebraska Territories to settle at the mouth of Echo Canyon in Utah Territory in 1854. He set up a station to trade with emigrants heading west on the Oregon Trail. In 1858 he went to work for the J. M. Hockaday and McGraw Stage Company when Hockaday was awarded the U.S. mail contract from Atchison, Kansas, to Salt Lake City. "I was put in charge of the road; I bought mules, built stations, fought Indians and did everything that came in the line of my duty. I started from Atchison and as I got one division in order, I was sent to the next, until finally, I was permanently located on the Salt Lake City division, having charge of the road from Pacific Springs to Salt Lake City." He continued ramrodding operations on that stretch of trail when Russell, Majors, and Waddell took over Hockaday's stage line.

Just as he had with all his previous employers, Bromley soon earned the respect and high regard of Russell. When Russell and his general superintendent, Benjamin Ficklin, sat down to work out the operating details of the Pony Express, they called in Bromley to help

Division Three superintendent James Bromley.

plan the route and determine the number of stations, horses, and riders that would be required. He was assigned the Division Three route from Elkhorn (Wyoming) in Nebraska Territory to Salt Lake City, a much longer division than when he ran the stage line for Hockaday. Bromley made his Weber station and home at the head of Echo Canyon his headquarters.

When the Pony Express ended, Bromley worked for "stagecoach king" Ben Holladay, who took over Russell, Majors, and Waddell's company. Then he tried his hand as a merchant and innkeeper. In 1868 Bromley sold his holdings at Echo Canyon to Brigham Young Jr. for two hundred dollars and set about designing Echo City. He died in 1888.

Following the River and Crossing the Plains

The trail of Bromley's Division Three Pony riders was long, dangerous, and spectacular. It followed the North Platte River from the mostly barren lands of the Great Plains to the Sweetwater River and the rugged passes of the Wasatch Range of the Rocky Mountains to the sunscorched valley of the Great Salt Lake. The division's westbound rider picked up the mail from Jack Slade's Division Two rider, galloped west toward Elkhorn, La Bonte, Bed Tick, La Prele, and Box Elder relays, then crossed the Deer Creek and Haystack Mountains, stopping at the Deer Creek station to hand over the mail to the next rider, who changed horses at Little Muddy and Bridger stations, then rode on to the Platte Bridge station.

HUTCHINGS' PANORAMIC SCENES.——CROSSING THE PLAINS.

EMIGRANT TRAIN PASSING WIND RIVER MOUNTAINS

SIOUX INDIANS

INDIANS CHASING BUFFALOES, SCOTT'S BLUFFS

STUCK FAST

COURT-HOUSE ROCK

FIRST NIGHT ON THE PLAINS

MOUTH of ASH HOLLOW

CHIMNEY ROCK

DEVIL'S GATE

LARAMIE PEAK

SCENE ON THE DESERT

CASTLE ROCK

Published by J. M. HUTCHINGS, Placerville. [Copyright secured.] DRIVING STOCK ACROSS THE PLAINS [Views drawn from Nature in 1855, by George H. Baker.

Newspaper broadsheet

The Bancroft Library, University of California, Berkley, California

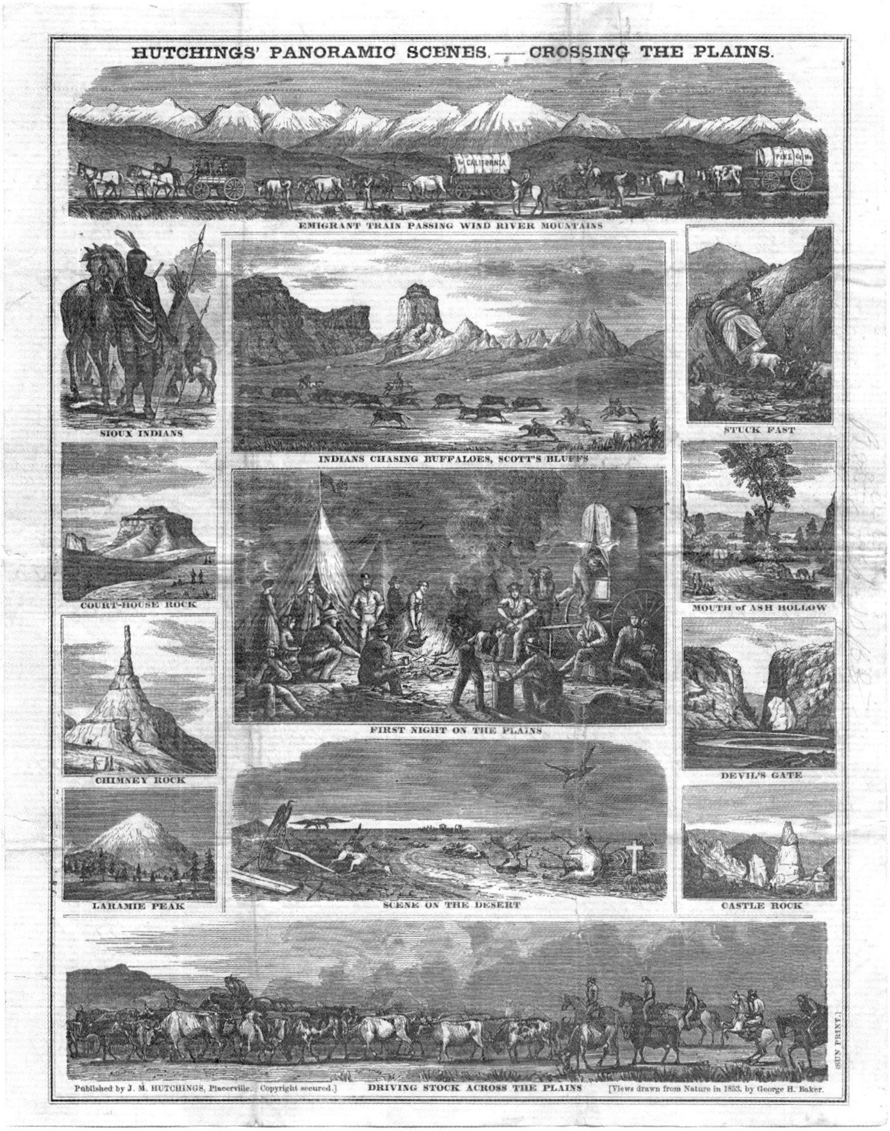

Guinard's Station complex, which included the Pony Express station, was renamed Fort Caspar in 1862. Bart Smith

Twenty-three years earlier, in 1847, Brigham Young's Pioneer Company had established a ferry service to float emigrants across the North Platte River on their "journey of hope" to Salt Lake City. Twelve years later, in 1859, Louis Guinard built a one-thousand-foot-long log toll bridge across the river and constructed a trading post. Near the bridge and trading post, Bromley built a stage and Pony Express station.

In 1862 Guinard's station complex was

Above, the Red Buttes west of Fort Caspar became the namesake for the Pony Express station built at the base of the Buttes. Bart Smith

Right, rider leaving Red Buttes Pony Express Station. Painting by W. H. Jackson. Courtesy Scotts Bluff National Monument

"Buffalo Bill" Cody

William F. Cody is listed as a Pony Express rider and claimed to be a rider between the Red Buttes and Three Crossings stations. There are numerous stories of his adventures. One story is certain: In 1857 eleven-year-old Billy Cody rode as a messenger for Russell, Majors, and Waddell carrying notes, instructions, and mail from one point to another around Leavenworth, Kansas. Other stories, laced with exciting adventures of Cody's exploits as a Pony rider, abound. Some may be true, like one that places him as a Pony rider who carried the mail on the perilous run between Red Buttes and Three Crossings. During one trip on his regular run, he was chased by Sioux Indians who "made it lively for the young messenger. But the speed and endurance of his steed soon told; lying flat on the animal's neck, he quickly distanced his assailants and thundered into Sweetwater, the next station, ahead of schedule. Here he found—as so often happened in the history of the express service—that the place had been raided, the keeper slain, and the horses driven off. There was nothing to do but drive his tired pony twelve miles further to Ploutz (Plants) Station where he got a fresh horse, briefly reported what he had observed and completed his run without mishap."

Other stories of Cody as a Pony Express rider include the time he made his run from Red Buttes to Three Crossings and found his relief rider had been killed in a fight the night before. He quickly mounted a fresh horse and headed for the Pacific Springs station, then returned with the eastbound mail to Red Buttes. This long, exhausting ride totaled somewhere between the 296 miles reported by some historians and the 388 miles calculated by others.

In another account of Cody's heroics as a Pony Express rider, he was carrying a mochila containing a large amount of money on the bandit-ridden run between Red Buttes and Three Crossings. Fearful that the bandits, or road agents as they were then called, would get wind of the contents of the pouch, he came up with a plan to fool them. He put the mochila containing the money under a saddle blanket and a mochila stuffed with paper over the saddle in the regular place. Two road agents stepped out from behind some rocks, leveled their guns at him, and demanded he turn over the mail pouch to them. He made a great show of protest and warned them of their no-doubt prompt demise if they insisted on confiscating the U.S. mail. The road agents promised Cody an even earlier demise if he didn't turn over the pouch. Cody loosened the mochila and threw it at the man nearest him. As the road agent ducked to escape the flying pouch, Cody drew his pistol, shot the other man, and spurred his horse into the first

Left to right, Colonel George A. Custer, a Russian Duke, and William Cody on a buffalo hunt. American Heritage Center, Laramie, Wyoming

bandit, knocking him to the ground. Then he galloped over the fallen man and away, arriving at the next station on time and with the mochila of money safely aboard his sweat-stained horse.

Christopher Corbett, in *Orphans Preferred*, challenges the truth of the stories of Cody as a Pony rider and sums up his assessment saying that "what seems probable is that Buffalo Bill invented this link with the Pony Express based on his brief experience as a messenger." In the long view of Pony Express history, it doesn't matter whether Cody's exploits were real or embellished truths or out-and-out fabrications, as the accounts of courage, stamina, and dedication and the dangers on the trail are rooted in the truths of Pony Express rides. They reflect the character of the riders who indeed endured such hardships, prevailed in similar adventures, and risked all to carry the mail through on time as a matter of personal honor.

occupied by the 11th Ohio Volunteer Cavalry to protect the telegraph line at Guinard's Bridge. The garrison was named "Mormon Ferry Post." It was later renamed Fort Caspar to honor Lieutenant Caspar Collins after his death in the 1865 Battle of Platte Bridge with the Sioux and Cheyenne.

Although most emigrants crossed the North Platte at the Mormon Ferry crossing or over Guinard's Bridge, many forded the river at the bend (now known as Bessemer Bend) instead of waiting in line and paying a toll to cross.

After crossing the Platte at the bend, the trail hugged the north bank of the river until it reached the Red Buttes station. On his stagecoach journey west, Sir Richard Burton described the Red Buttes that loomed on the horizon: "The feature from which it derives its name lies on the right bank of and about five miles distant from, the river, which here cuts its way through a ridge. These bluffs are a fine bold formation, escarpment of ruddy argillaceous sandstone, and shells, which dip toward the west; they are the eastern wall of the mass that hems in the stream, and rear high above it their conical heads and fantastic figures." The station at the base of the Red Buttes was both a stage stop and a Pony Express relay. Although Red Buttes is identified as a relay station, it became famous as the home station of "Buffalo Bill" Cody and an anchoring landmark for his tales of adventures as a Pony Express rider.

Riding the Rough, Dry Country of the Sweetwater River

It may have been young Billy Cody or another Pony rider who threw the *mochila* on the saddle of the fresh mount taken from the corrals of the Red Buttes relay and rode on to the home station at Willow Spring. The relief rider at Willow Spring took the *mochila*, slapped it across his saddle, and galloped up the steep trail that brought him and his sweat-lathered horse into the relay at Horse Creek. A hearty hello and a quick change of mounts and the rider was on his way up the trail, pulling in for a change of horses at the sorry shack and horse shed that served as the relay station near the base of Independence Rock.

Independence Rock was so called because many wagon trains reached it around the Fourth of July and celebrated there. But it is more famous as the "Great Record of the Desert." Early fur trappers and explorers carved their names on the nearly flat top of the granite monolith, and the thousands of emigrants that followed chiseled their names, the date, and sometimes a message about their westbound journey.

Inscriptions atop Independence Rock.
Bart Smith

Pony riders used Devil's Gate as a landmark but avoided riding through the narrow canyon. Bart Smith

The Independence Rock station, which was also known as the Sweetwater station, was abandoned about six months after the Pony Express started. Riders possibly used a station farther west, near Devil's Gate where the Sweetwater River cuts through a cleft in a narrow canyon. Neither wagons nor stagecoaches nor Pony Express riders traveled through Devil's Gate, but some emigrants are known to have walked through the gorge, exploring the canyon while their wagons lumbered along the trail that detoured around it.

Remains of the Three Crossing Pony Express Station taken in 1870 by W. H. Jackson, who a decade earlier painted renditions of many of the Pony Express Stations. Scotts Bluff National Monument

Farther along the trail the Pony rider came to the Split Rock stage and relay station at the base of Split Rock. This oddly shaped massive pile of rock in the Sweetwater Valley could be seen east and west for miles and was a landmark guide for Indians, trappers, and emigrants to the twenty-mile-wide South Pass through the Rocky Mountains. Mountain man James Clyman wrote in his 1844 journal, "This region seems to be the rufuses of the world thrown up in the utmost confusion."

After leaving Split Rock the rider followed the Sweetwater River, crossing its switchback turns three times before reaching the home station aptly named Three Crossings. The next rider took off with the mail pouch, climbing the dusty trail toward the grassy swamp of Ice Slough near the crest of the Continental Divide. Here a bed of ice lay about a foot underneath the sod. The keepers at the Ice Slough Pony Express relay well

Pony rider pulling into the Rocky Ridge (St. Mary) station while a stock tender holds a fresh horse for the relay. Painting by W. H. Jackson. Courtesy Scotts Bluff National Monument

The Rocky Ridge station was better known by Pony riders as St. Mary's and may have been a home station. It was located east of where the trail climbed through a rugged rocky path to the barren rocky ridges and then through the twenty-mile-wide notch in the Rocky Mountain wall known as South Pass.

The South Pass Pony Express Station was first known as Gilbert's station and Upper Sweetwater station, and following the war with the Sioux and Cheyenne, when it was burned to the ground in 1868, it was known as Burnt Ranch. After changing horses

enjoyed the food-keeping and drink-cooling benefits of their station, and emigrants and stagecoach drivers chopped off chunks of the ice to cool their water casks as they journeyed onward during the hot summer months. Pony riders also enjoyed a quick gulp of cool water as they mounted a fresh horse and headed west toward the Rocky Ridge station.

at the South Pass relay, the rider spurred his horse into a run through the broad grassy meadow of South Pass and over the Continental Divide and on toward the Pacific Springs station.

Beyond Pacific Springs, at "Parting of the Ways," the trail dropped southwest to Fort Bridger. Emigrants on the trail who were headed for Oregon had to make a choice: Should they take the safer, well-watered, long-used route to Fort Bridger and then head northwest again, or should they continue straight west on the nearly fifty-mile shorter route across the waterless, grassless tablelands of graveled rifts and dried-up alkali lakes, where the bleached bones of cattle and oxen of earlier emigrants had died of thirst along the way to the Green River? The shorter, hazardous

The Pony Express station was near the remaining buildings in Pacific Springs. Bart Smith

route was pioneered in 1844 by a wagon train guided by Caleb Greenwood and first known as the Greenwood Cutoff. But then due to an error in Joseph Ware's 1849 *The Emigrants' Guide to California*, it became known as the Sublette Cutoff for Solomon Sublette, who had told Ware about the shortcut. (This cutoff starts about nine and half miles west-southwest of the "Parting of the Ways" marker on the Pony Express Trail.)

There was no such angst for the Overland stages or the Pony Express riders. Their trail, which they knew well, followed the old Oregon Trail that crossed the Green River and Hams Fork to Fort Bridger, then dipped southwest to Salt Lake. There were three Pony Express relays—Big Sandy, Big Timber, and Big Bend between the Greenwood-Sublette Cutoff and where the trail crossed the Green River at the Green River station. In summertime, when the River dropped to about three feet deep, it was fordable. But after heavy rains the swift running waters of the Green could be safely crossed only by ferry. According to one pioneer, the ferry that took them across near the Green River station used "a very unsafe flat boat, a heavy wagon comes near sinking it, for which they charge $4 per wagon but there is no help for it." He went on to explain, "It required one man to bail all the time, while another at every trip kept stuffing in bits of rag." Wild river ride or not, the Pony Express rider urged his horse to clop aboard the ferry, and when it reached the other side, the still-mounted rider jumped the animal off and spurred him into a hard run toward the relays at Martin's station, Ham's Fork, and Church Buttes before coming into Fort Bridger.

Jim Bridger's Fort

Fort Bridger was the home of mountain man and trailblazer Jim Bridger, who had roamed the Rockies as a fur trapper since 1822. He was among the great adventurers—Jedediah Smith, James Clyman, Tomas Fitzpatrick, Joe Meek, and Joe Walker—who first explored the mountains and passes, rivers and streams, and deserts and wastelands hidden in the vastness of the American West. Bridger claimed he discovered the Great Salt Lake and often told the story of how it happened. He and a party of trappers were camped a little west of what is now the Wyoming border in 1825. Two of the trappers made a wager about the course of the Bear River, which flowed near their camp. Bridger decided to settle the bet and ran the river in a bull boat (a boat made of willows and covered with bison hides) to where it

Deteriorating buildings of the South Bend Stage Station in Granger, Wyoming. This stage station was near the Ham's Fork station and was similar to stations used by the Pony Express. Bart Smith

flowed into what appeared to be an immense shallow bay. He tasted the water and found it salty. Believing that he had found an arm of the Pacific Ocean, he returned to camp with the story of his discovery. We don't know who won the bet.

In 1830 Bridger and a group of trappers established the Rocky Mountain Fur Company, and in 1843 he and fellow trapper Louis Vasquez built the trading post that was later named Fort Bridger to sell supplies and trade rested oxen to emigrants for cash and their broken-down animals that just came off the South Pass. They hastily built their fort, and like its rugged owners, it was neither finely crafted nor endowed with comforts. It was built of logs daubed with sun-baked mud and described by emigrant Joel Palmer as a ". . . shabby concern. Here are about twenty-five lodges of Indians, or rather white trapper's lodges occupied by their Indian wives. They have a good supply of robes, dressed deer, elk and antelope skins, coats, plants, moccasins, and other Indian fixens, which they trade low for flour, pork, powder, lead, blankets, butcher-knives, hats, ready-made clothes, coffee, sugar, etc. . . ." Emigrant and later Pony Express rider Howard Egan, the son of Division Four's supervisor of the same name, described the fort as, "Low dirt covered houses near the bank of the river. Indians and white men all dressed in buckskin clothes, and more dogs, half-bred wolf, than you could shake a stick at."

Though somewhat settled in at the fort, in 1850 the itchy foot of the trailblazer sent Bridger on a quest to find an alternate route to South Pass that shortened the Oregon Trail by sixty-one miles. Eight years later he sold the fort, and in 1864 the sixty-year-old frontiersman blazed the Bridger Trail—an alternate route from Wyoming to Montana that avoided the bloody Bozeman Trail. He served as a scout for the army during the Powder River Expedition against the Sioux and Cheyenne. In 1868 Bridger, stricken with arthritis and rheumatism, returned to his Missouri roots and died in Washington, Missouri, in 1881.

The Downhill Ride from the Rockies to the Great Basin

After leaving Fort Bridger, the Pony Express rider changed horses again at Muddy Creek, Quaking Asp, and the last station in the Rockies, the Bear River station. He then headed southwest into Utah Territory, winding his way through the high hills of the Uinta Mountains to Needle Rock relay, and then eight more miles to the home station at the head of the twenty-mile-long Echo Canyon.

The relay rider out of Echo Canyon changed horses at the Halfway station before traveling on through the canyon walled by six-thousand-foot-high mountains. This was a tough run in the winter, when biting, snow-blinding winds howled through the canyon and piled up snow, and it was not much better in summer, when the heat trapped by the canyon walls made the trail hot as an oven. Cold or hot, the Pony rider rode on, reaching the Weber station, where Division three superintendent James Bromley had his headquarters.

With a fresh horse under him, the rider bolted from the Weber relay, crossed the Weber River at Forney's Bridge, and then began the steep climb up Bachelor's Canyon to Dixie Hollow. When the canyon was snowed in, the rider rode down the valley to the Henneferville emergency station and around by Little East Canyon to Dixie Hollow. Eight miles more and he was at Wheaton Springs, changing horses for another eight-mile ride to Mountain Dale.

Rider George Edwin Little's daughter recalled the day when her father was bringing in the mail from the east to Salt Lake during a heavy

Pony rider and horse struggling through a blinding blizzard to carry the mail through to the next station. Department of State Parks and Cultural Resources, Cheyenne, Wyoming

snowstorm. The snow became so heavy and deep that his horse gave out and he had to leave him. He used his pocketknife to cut the mail pouches open and stuffed the mail inside his shirt. He then broke trail to Mountain Dale, arriving about 3 a.m. When daylight broke, he mounted a fresh horse and rode over Little Mountain, past Donner Hill and Emigrant Canyon and into the valley of the Great Salt Lake, where he handed the mail over to the Division Four relief rider and strolled into the Salt Lake House home station.

Legendary Mormon scout Howard Egan managed Pony Express operations from Trader's Rest to Robert's Creek. His Division Four headquarters was in Salt Lake City.

7

CROSSING THE GREAT BASIN

Howard Egan had charge of the stage and Pony Express operations in the salt plains, deserts, and mountains of the Great Basin—a stretch of trail across land that a little over two decades earlier was forsaken as desolate and uninhabitable. Westbound emigrants struggled to put it behind them, and many died trying. But in 1847 Brigham Young, who inherited leadership of Joseph Smith's Mormon Church, laid claim to this land that no one wanted and organized a mass march of his followers from their persecution in Ohio, Missouri, and Illinois to their "earthly Eden" in the Great Salt Lake Valley. Young's pioneers put their might together and built dams, flumes, and a system of canals to bring water from the mountain lakes and canyons to grow their city and irrigate the sterile lands of the plains and deserts for farming. By 1860 Salt Lake City was a frontier metropolis of houses, busy stores, liveries, blacksmith shops, and hotels. Salt Lake House was a favored stop for stage passengers Horace Greeley, Sir Richard Burton, and Mark Twain, easterners who relished a bath, clean beds, and excellent food. Salt Lake House was also acclaimed as the most comfortable home station east of St. Joseph for Pony Express riders.

Egan, an Ireland-born emigrant from Canada, had a successful rope-making business in Illinois and became a Mormon. He served as a major in Young's Nauvoo Legion militia and helped lead the first three wagon trains of Mormon migration to Utah in 1847, 1848, and 1849. On his last trip Egan was accompanied by his wives and children, including eight-year-old Howard Ransom and six-year-old Richard Eurastus (Ras), who would later ride

Salt Lake City, ca. 1866. Historical Department of the Church of Jesus Christ of Latter-day Saints

for the Pony Express. Egan settled in Utah Territory and scouted the country from Salt Lake City to California.

While driving a herd of cattle from California to start herds and fill bellies in Utah, Egan discovered a shorter route across Nevada than the oft used Humboldt River Route to the north. This shorter route, known as the Egan Trail, was used by George W. Chorpenning's 1858 stage and mail service between Salt Lake City and Placerville,

California. When Russell, Major, and Waddell took over Chorpenning's company in 1860 and established the Central Overland California and Pikes Peak Express Company and launched the Pony Express, they put Egan in charge of operations of Division Four.

After his days with the Pony Express, Egan established a store in Ruby Valley and several businesses in Salt Lake City. He sold beef to placer miners in California, mined his own claims in the Deep Creek Mountains, and founded the town of Deep Creek in the Ibapah Valley. Egan, Egan Trail, the Egan station, and Egan Canyon are all named for the legendary Mormon scout, stage and Pony Express superintendent, and businessman. He died in 1878 following an illness (probably pneumonia) he contracted while guarding Young's grave.

Riding the Trail to Camp Floyd

Porter Rockwell, known as "Port" or "Old Port," doubled as the territorial marshal and operated Rockwell's relay station. He was a loyal follower of the Mormon faith and was both honored and vilified as one of the "Destroying Angels." Destroying Angels, as Mark Twain understood it and reported in *Roughing It,* "are Latter-day Saints who are set apart by the Church to conduct permanent disappearances of obnoxious citizens." Twain had supper with Rockwell and described him as "a loud, profane, offensive old blackguard" but seemed to like him.

Rockwell was born in Belcher, Massachusetts, in 1813, baptized into the Church of Jesus Christ of Latter-day Saints in New York in 1830, and moved to Missouri that same year. He was believed to have been a member of the "Danites," a Mormon vigilante group who organized in 1838 to defend fellow church members against their enemies following Missouri governor Lilburn Boggs's notorious executive order stating that "the Mormons must be treated as enemies and must be exterminated or driven from the State if necessary for the public peace. . . ." In 1842 Rockwell was accused of attempting to assassinate Lilburn Boggs and was jailed for nine months while awaiting his trial. The grand jury reported that there wasn't sufficient evidence to indict Rockwell—possibly convinced by his reputation as a gunman and his statement that he "never shot at anybody, if I shoot they get shot! . . . He's still alive, ain't he?"

Rockwell came west with Brigham Young in 1847, settling in the Salt Lake Valley, and was appointed deputy marshal for Young's 1849

Frontier Justice

Irishman Howard Egan was baptized a Mormon in 1842 and two years later began to practice the Mormon doctrine of polygamy. In addition to his first wife, Tamson Parshley, whom he had married in 1838, he was sealed (married) to Cathrine Clawson in 1844, Nancy Redding in 1846, and Mary Egan in 1848. Upon his return from his 1849 trip to lead a train of Mormons to Salt Lake City, Brigham Young immediately sent Egan on another mission—to guide a company of forty-niners to California. When Egan returned to Salt Lake in 1850, he discovered that James Monroe had seduced one of his wives and she had given birth to Monroe's child.

Whether Egan was acquainted with Monroe is unknown. Monroe was originally from Utica, New York, and was living in Utah and was a Mormon or former Mormon. Egan set out to avenge the seduction of his wife, or as some writers of the day wrote, "hunt Monroe down like a dog." In September 1851 Egan rode toward Fort Bridger. A few miles west of Bear River, he met up with the wagon train that Monroe was traveling with and promptly shot him.

Apparently Egan turned himself over to the law, and a few days later a Mormon hearing was held and the murder case against him dismissed. Two weeks after the Mormon hearing, the matter was brought to the U.S. District Court for the Territory of Utah. George A. Smith, the attorney for Egan's defense, boldly argued, "All I want is simply truth and justice. This defendant asks not his life, if he deserves to die; but if he has done nothing but an act of justice, he wishes that justice awarded to him." He went on to argue that Monroe "seduced Egan's wife; that he had come into this place in the absence of her husband, and had seduced his family, in consequence of which, an illegitimate child had been brought into the world; and the disgrace which must arise from such a transaction in his family, had fallen on the head of the defendant." Then Smith went on to explain, "In England when a man seduces the wife or relative the injured enters a civil suit for damages . . . and may get twenty pounds as damages. In this case, character is not estimated, neither reputation, but the number of pounds, shillings and pence alone bear the sway, which is common in courts of all old and rotten governments. In taking this point into consideration I argue that in this territory it is a principle of mountain common law, that no man can seduce the wife of another without endangering his own life." Smith summed up his defense with, "I come before you, not for the pence of that gentlemen, the defendant, but to plead for the honor and rights of the whole people, and the defendant in particular; and, gentlemen of the jury, with the limited knowledge I have of law, were I a juryman I would lie in the jury room until the worms should draw me through the key-hole before I would give in my verdict to hang a man for doing an act of justice, for the neglect of which he would have been damned in the eyes of this whole community."

Fifteen minutes after the jury received the case for deliberation, they returned a verdict of "Not guilty."

The following March the Utah Territorial legislature passed the Justifiable Homicide Act, which made killing the person who defiled a wife, daughter, mother, sister, or any other female relative or dependent justifiable. The law was enforced until 1874, when it was changed by the U.S. Congress.

—Partially excerpted from court
records and The History of
Utah by Orson Ferguson Whitney.

Pony riders enjoyed the comforts of the home station in Salt Lake House.

provisional state of Deseret, which included all of present-day Utah and Nevada and parts of California, Colorado, New Mexico, Wyoming, Idaho, and Oregon. Young's grand plan was eventually whittled down by the U.S. Congress and became known as Utah Territory, which included what is now Utah, Nevada, and parts of Wyoming and Colorado. Rockwell remained as marshal of Utah Territory. In 1857–1858 he was among the Nauvoo Legion militia sent by Young to delay U.S. troops from entering the territory during what was then termed the "Mormon Rebellion" or Utah War.

There were many more stories on the frontier of Rockwell's exploits as gunman, lawman, militiaman, and avenger. Fitz Hugh Ludlow, noted journalist and explorer who traveled across America on the Overland stage, described Rockwell "as a powerful physical nature welded to a mind of very narrow perceptions, intense convictions and changeless tenacity. In his build he was a gladiator, in his humor a Yankee lumberman; in his memory a Bourbon; in his vengeance an Indian. A strange mixture, only to be found on the American continent." Rockwell died of natural causes in 1878. The former site of Rockwell's station is now on the grounds of the state prison, and a nearby stone marker commemorates the location.

"Port" Rockwell—territorial marshal, Old West legend and Pony Express station keeper. Used by permission, Utah State Historical Society, all rights reserved

Eleven miles past Rockwell's, the Pony rider pulled into Joe's Dugout. The dugout that gave Joe Dorton's station its name was where a young Indian stock tender lived. The station actually consisted of a two-room brick house, a log barn, and a grocery store. Water was brought in by pack mule from Utah Lake and sold for twenty-five cents a bucket.

Willow tree planted in 1858 in back of the Carson's Inn station. Bart Smith

The next stage and Pony Express station was at John Carson's Inn in the flourishing city of Fairfield, where nearly four thousand people resided. Fairfield was adjacent to the U.S. Army's Camp Floyd, which was established in 1858 during the Utah War and garrisoned three thousand troops. Once the situation with the Mormons was settled, the troops were ordered to protect emigrants, settlers, and station keepers from attack by Indians and white bandits disguised as Indians. One such order issued to Lieutenant John Green of the Second Dragoons was found in the National Archives by Richard Fike. It made it clear, "Should the least resistance be offered you in the discharge of this duty, you will not hesitate to exterminate the rascals."

Camp Floyd was named for Secretary of War John B. Floyd, and the name was changed to Fort Crittenden when its namesake joined the Confederacy. The fort was abandoned in 1861, and the troops were sent east to fight in the Civil War. Shortly after the troops left for the east, the thriving city of Fairfield dwindled to eighteen families. The adobe building of the Carson Inn Pony Express Station is still standing and is open to the public. Its location is part of Utah State Park.

The Trail through "Paiute Hell"

The trail beyond Camp Floyd passed through No Name Pass and Faust's Rush Valley station, rose to Point Lookout, and then dropped into the high desert of the Great Basin, where it crossed a series of long, wide, desolate valleys separated by narrow north-south trending mountain ridges—a land known by the early settlers as "Paiute Hell." It was brutally hot in summer, bone-piercing cold

Pony Express rider fleeing approaching Indians. Painting by W. H. Jackson. Courtesy Scotts Bluff National Monument

Pony Express rider Richard Erastus Egan.
Courtesy The St. Joseph Museums, Inc., St. Joseph, Missouri

in winter, and, for the nineteen months of the Pony Express, a no-man's land of desperate Indians and white invaders.

The Rush Valley station was built in 1858 for George Chorpenning's "Jackass " mail company. Henry Jacob "Doc" Faust, who helped Howard Egan organize the Division Four route, purchased the land as a ranch to raise horses for the Pony Express and serve as a home station for riders. The station quickly became known as Faust's or Doc Faust's.

Faust never completed his studies in medicine but knew enough to set broken bones; lance, patch, and stitch wounds; and dig out a bullet or arrow if it wasn't too close to something vital.

He treated many riders, stage passengers, local Indians, and settlers as much for diseases and ailments as for wounds. He was well known on the frontier, and in Utah Faust is famous for bringing in the first blooded cattle stock to Utah and organizing the Utah Cattle Convention. He lived at the station until 1870, then sold his stock and holdings in Rush Valley and went into the livery business in Salt Lake City. He died in 1904.

One of the riders from Doc Faust's station at Rush Valley was Howard Egan's son Richard Erastus "Ras" Egan. He was hired by his father to make the Express run from the headquarters at Salt Lake City to Doc Faust's. In the winter of 1860, Ras made the run as far as the Carson Inn relay near Camp Floyd, changed horses, and headed toward Doc Faust's station during a blinding snowstorm. When darkness fell, it was impossible to see the trail. Ras reasoned that if he kept the wind at his right cheek as he traveled all night, he would be moving in the direction of Doc Faust's station. At dawn he discovered that the wind had changed during the night and he had ridden 150 miles in a wide circle; he was back where he started at Camp Floyd. Galled by his error, but true to his oath as a Pony Express rider, he called for a fresh horse and started out again for Doc Faust's station. The mail had to keep moving.

Once the Pony rider left Doc Faust's station, he climbed to Point Lookout, then dropped to the desolate lands that skirted the southern border of the Great Salt Lake Desert. In the summer months, sunburned and sweat-drenched Pony riders changed their weary ponies for rested horses at relay stations that could only be described as miserable. In winter the country was as freezing cold and windblown as it had been hot in summer. Sir Richard Burton described the stations along this stretch of trail as "a hard life, setting aside the chance of death — no less than three murders have been committed by the Indians during this year — the work is severe; the diet is sometimes reduced

A herd of wild horses seen from the Pony Express Trail near Simpson's Spring station. Bart Smith

to wolf-mutton, or a little boiled wheat and rye, and the drink to brackish water; a pound of tea comes occasionally, the droughty souls are always 'out' of whiskey and tobacco."

Life on the trail for Pony Express riders only partly matched the hardships experienced by station keepers. They bunked at home stations, ate the food, drank the brackish water, suffered the heat and cold, but had the advantage of being on the move. They were a wind on the desert, coming and going, waving at stages, galloping in on fast horses, leaping off, tossing the *mochila* on another mount, and taking off again to the next station. They were making history.

A tortuous trail led from Doc Faust's to the Simpson's Springs station, but there was a spring of good water nearby to quench the rider's thirst before going on. Horace Greeley stopped here in 1859 and lamented, "I fear the hot suns of August will dry up this spring—while there is no other fit to drink for a weary distance south and west of this place."

This station, as were others along the trail, was originally built for Chorpenning's "Jackass" mail company's mule-drawn wagons and was then used as a way and relay station for Concord stagecoaches and Pony Express riders when Russell, Majors, and Waddell took over Chorpenning's company.

The relay rider who carried the mail from the home station at Faust's had ridden twenty-four miles through burning desert and had nearly another thirty-three miles to go before reaching the next home station at Fish Springs. Along the trail the rider changed horses at the Riverbed, Dugway, and Black Rock stations. At Riverbed it was always a guess as to who would be there to ready the relay horse. Strange, eerie sounds traveled through this station, making it difficult to keep station keepers and stock tenders. At least three station keepers left after hearing the sounds of "desert fairies."

The Dugway station, ten miles farther, amounted to a large hole with a shelter, adobe chimney, and wooden front door stuck on it. Water was hauled from Simpson's Springs. Stage passenger Greeley described Dugway as "about the forlornest spot I ever saw." Just as forlorn was the Black Rock station fourteen miles west.

The ride from the Dugway station to Black Rock was over the steep Dugway Pass, referred to by some as "break-neck hill." Emigrants heading west over this steep hill wisely dug a trench along the uphill side of the mountain. They rolled their uphill-side wagon wheels into the dugway (trench) to keep their wagons from tipping over and tumbling down the canyon as the oxen pulled them up and over the pass.

Tumbling off the trail was not a particular hazard for the sure-footed ponies of the Express riders, but the dreaded pass was one of the more dangerous places for an ambush by Indians or bandits. There was at least one report of a rider who rode through the pass at a dead run with Indians in hot pursuit and arrows whizzing so close by his head he could feel the wind from them on his neck.

The forlorn Black Rock station was not much

Winter snows blanket the restored Simpson Springs Pony Express Station at Simpson Springs, Utah. The station was named for Captain J. H. Simpson, who camped here in 1858 while searching for the overland mail route to California. Bart Smith

Early photo of Fish Springs station.

to look forward to after coming down from Dugway Pass. The station was built of rock, probably black volcanic rock from the nearby outcrop, and the land was harsh, barren, and bone dry. Upon seeing Rock Creek Mark Twain wrote, ". . . not a living creature visible in any direction whither one searches the bland level that stretches its monotonous miles on every hand." Water for the attendant, horses, stage passengers, and Pony riders was hauled in barrels from Boyd's station farther west.

About ten miles beyond Black Rock, the weary rider pulled up at the home station at Fish

Remnants of Boyd's Pony Express Station east of Callao, Utah. Remaining walls of Boyd's station reveal bunk bed slats where riders slept. Bart Smith

Willow Springs Pony Express Station was purchased by the David C. Bagley family in 1886 and still operates as the Bagley Ranch. *Courtesy Don and Beth Anderson and David C. Bagley family*

Springs station, where he handed the mail pouch over to another rider. Riding into Fish Springs was akin to suddenly finding an oasis in the Sahara. It was near warm spring-fed marshes and pools of clear water filled with chub fish and migrating swans, geese, ducks, herons, pelicans, and avocets. The marshes are fed by underground water that was once part of prehistoric Lake Bonneville. A gentleman named Smith, of whom little is known, operated the native stone station. What became of the station is also unknown, but the site is now part of the Fish Springs National Wildlife Refuge.

The relief rider from Fish Springs tucked the westbound *mochila* safely under him and took one of two trails. In good weather he rode nine miles through the pass over the Fish Springs Range. If bad, he rode an extra five miles, taking a trail around the north end of the mountain range to Boyd's station.

George Washington Boyd's station was a small log and stone structure built in about 1855. Boyd was apparently a cautious man and built rifle ports into the structure on all four sides. The gun ports came in handy when the station was attacked in 1860—only three horses were stolen and some hay burned. Boyd, who had also built the Willow Springs, Fish Springs, Black Rock, and Dugway stations for Howard Egan, was also

Fortifications against Indians above Cañon station near Callao, Utah. Bart Smith

Remains of Cañon Station being examined by rancher David Bagley and his father, "Grandpa" Cyrene, whose family still owns the Willow Springs Station Ranch. Courtesy Don and Beth Anderson and David C. Bagley family

under contract to Egan to haul hay, wood, and water to the Black Rock and Dugway stations.

From Boyd's the rider headed eight miles west to the Willow Springs station, changed horses, and rode six miles to Willow Creek. Historians and archeologists are still debating the existence of a Willow Creek station, but whether there was a relay station at Willow Creek or not, the rider went another six miles to the Cañon station.

The Cañon station was another desert

dugout with a stable and barn and possibly a log house. Historians are not sure exactly where Egan built the station. It was near Overland or Blood Canyon or possibly on Clifton Flat. Two years after the era of the Pony Express, Indians attacked the station, which was still a stage stop. Egan described the attack in his memoirs: "The Indians waited till the men had been called to breakfast in the dugout, and were all down in the hole without guns, all except the hostler, William Riley, who was currying a horse just outside the south door of the stable at the time of the first alarm, and he was shot through the ankle and bone broken short off. He started down the canyon on the run, but did not get very far before he was caught and killed." Egan went on to write, "The men at breakfast were mostly all killed as they came out of the dugout to reach their arms that were staked in the south end of the barn. Not one of them ever reached his gun. One man, though wounded, tried to excape by running down the canyon as Riley did. He got further away, but was caught and killed, and, as he was some bald on top of his head, and a good growth of whiskers on his chin, they scalped that and left him where he fell."

After the attack the station became known as the Burnt station and another, more defensible stage station was built above the mouth of Overland Canyon.

A fourteen-mile ride through Overland Canyon brought the Pony Express rider to the home station at Deep Creek, where Egan's family lived. They farmed the land around Deep Creek, raising hay and grain for the Fish Springs, Black Rock, and Boyd's station Pony Express relays east of them. They also operated a general store at this location. It could have been a moneymaker for the Egan's, but Tamson, Egan's first wife, freely handed out food, supplies, and clothing to Indians, emigrants, and stage travelers who did not have money or something to trade in exchange for the goods they received.

The Deep Creek station was the last station in what would later be the state of Utah. (When the Pony Express started in the spring of 1860, Nevada was still part of Utah Territory. But a year later, in March 1861, Nevada Territory was established, which included the western three-quarters of the eventual state of Nevada.)

Riding through the "Damndest Country under the Sun"

On his overland stage journey west to Carson Valley in 1861, Mark Twain once heard a man refer to Nevada as the "damndest country under the sun" and quite agreed with him. Pony Express riders riding the nearly five hundred miles of harsh, winding trail across the sagebrush- and greasewood-dotted deserts and mountains of Nevada in the Great Basin may well have thought so too. Their job was to cross the deserts as quickly as they could, and most Euro-American travelers of the 1800s were of the same notion. But the Western Shoshone and Paiute claimed the deserts of the Great Basin as their territorial grounds and had no wish to leave.

For thousands of years the Shoshone and Paiute had subsisted on the sparse resources of the desert by hunting antelope and rabbit, rounding up grasshoppers and rodents, and harvesting seeds, nuts, berries, and roots. They knew where to find water even during the driest of times. In the 1840s and 1850s, their way of life began to change. Forty-niners were rushing across the continent to the goldfields of California. Mormons were settling as far into Nevada and California as they could manage. In 1859 silver was discovered in the Washoe Hills of Nevada, and miners poured into the country with the same zeal they went after gold a decade earlier.

A chain of Overland stage and Pony Express stations dotted the country. These newcomers to the Nevada deserts understandably settled near water sources whenever they could. They cut down pinion trees for fuel, and their stock trampled or ate the sparse vegetation. These were the same resources the Shoshone and Paiute depended on for survival. They partly adapted to the change by trading their finely woven baskets and antelope and rabbit skins for food and goods. Kindly settlers sometimes gave them food and blankets. Some Shoshone and Paiute took jobs farming for the settlers or served as stock tenders at the stage and Pony Express stations, and others scouted for the army. Nevertheless, they resented the encroachment into their territory, and there were bound to be conflicts. However it was not the deep-seated resentment or the increasing encroachment that set off the Paiute War of 1860; it was the rape of a Paiute woman at Williams station in Division Five's Carson Valley.

The Pony Express was only a month old when the Paiute War began, and once it started no Pony rider, station keeper, stock tender, stage driver, passenger, trader, or settler could rest easy. Angered Paiute and Shoshone were joined by equally hostile Goshute and Bannocks and commenced raiding remote stations in Nevada and Utah.

Riders leaving Egan's Deep Creek station heading west had a long run of fifteen miles before

Rubble and foundation are all that remain of the Antelope Springs station. Bart Smith

reaching the Antelope Springs station. (Later the Prairie Gate station was built eight miles from Deep Creek.) Two months after the Pony Express started, Antelope Springs was burned by Paiutes.

Farther west was the Spring Valley station, which was used during the final months of the Pony Express, and beyond there was the home station at Schell Creek.

The Schell Creek station was built in 1859 by Chorpenning and Egan for Chorpenning's "Jackass" mail operation. Shortly after it was built, cavalry troops from Camp Floyd were garrisoned there to protect emigrants who were crossing the desert to California and the flood of hopefuls on their way to search for silver and gold in the hills around Virginia City's Comstock Lode. The station became known as Fort Schellbourne. A fierce battle between soldiers and Paiute warriors took place at the fort during the 1860 conflict.

When the era of the Pony Express came to a close, Schellbourne continued to serve as a stage station for Ben Holladay's Overland Mail and Express Company until 1869. In 1870 silver was discovered in the nearby mountains, and Schellbourne was instantly turned into a rip-roaring mining camp of nearly five hundred people. The mines played out about 1885, and the desert mining camp dwindled to a ghost town. The ghostly remnants of Schellbourne are now part of a privately owned ranch.

West of the bullet-scarred Schellbourne station, the Pony Express rider thundered through the steep, high, rugged mountains of Egan Canyon to Egan station in the "very pretty little valley about a half mile across either way," wrote Pony rider William F. "Billy" Fisher while scribbling in his diary about the August 1860 Goshute attack at the station.

On the morning of August 11, station keeper Mike Holton and Pony rider Nick Wilson were the only two people at Egan station. A large band of armed Goshutes rode through the canyon, surrounded the station, and demanded that the station keeper give them all the food stores. Outnumbered and outgunned, Holton and Wilson handed out the food. They then started out to gather the Pony Express horses into the corral but were ordered to get back in the station. Holton and Wilson, expecting to be "massacred by the murderous red devils," barricaded the door and window with grain sacks, leaving space to aim their rifles, and waited for the attack.

Meanwhile, Pony rider William Dennis, on his run east from the relay at Butte station, was riding through Nipcut Canyon. As he entered the valley, he saw the Indians before they caught sight of him and whirled his pony around and headed back to alert a detachment of U.S. Army troops that he had passed earlier. Dennis found the troops (three sergeants and twenty-four privates) about a mile down the trail and gave a quick report to the commanding officer, First Lieutenant Stephen Weed. Weed put a sergeant in charge of seven men and two supply wagons and led the

Egan's Canyon was described as "grand, solemn and impressive" by army trooper Charles A. Scott, and traveler Sir Richard Burton wrote, "an uglier place for sharp shooting can hardly be imagined." Bart Smith

rest of his detachment to the Egan station. "I gave directions for surrounding the Indians near the station, and while that was being executed two or three of my men too eager to commence fired prematurely, thus alarming the Indians and leaving them an opportunity to retreat, which they lost no time in taking advantage of; the fire then became general, but the Indians got up the mountains south and east of the station where they were well protected from our fire by rocks and trees." The

Indians fired a couple of volleys at the soldiers, then disappeared over the horizon. In Weed's report, dispatched to the adjutant general at Camp Floyd the next morning, he wrote that three of his men were wounded—two seriously—and that one Indian was killed and three wounded. Six of Weed's troopers were mentioned for their "meritorious conduct during the skirmish." Weed sent

Utah Territory Pony Express riders, left to right, John Fisher, John Hancock, and William F. "Billy" Fisher. Fisher rode 300 miles in thirty hours, using eight horses to warn the stations between Ruby Valley and Salt Lake City that the Indians were on the attack.

Courtesy The St. Joseph Museums, Inc., St. Joseph, Missouri

Pony Express rider Elijah Nichols "Uncle Nick" Wilson rode between Deep Creek and Shell Station. He had lived with the Shoshones for two years as a youth and grew up a frontiersman to the bone. After his days with the Pony Express, he settled near Wilson, Wyoming, a town named in his honor, and wrote his autobiography, *The White Indian Boy: The Story of Uncle Nick Among the Shoshones.* Courtesy The St. Joseph Museums, Inc., St. Joseph, Missouri

Native-American petroglyphs a half mile from the Pony Express Trail along the route between Egan and Robert's Creek Stations. Bart Smith

**Pony Express
Trail east across
Diamond Springs
Valley.** Bart Smith

an eight-man escort and his wounded to the Ruby Valley station to get medical attention, and he also sent a small party of troops to escort east-bound Pony rider Dennis through Egan Canyon. He and eleven of his men stayed at the station to wait for "that portion of the company which can be spared from Ruby Valley, when I shall go to Antelope Springs."

In early fall the Indians returned, killed the station attendants, and burned the station. When Richard Burton passed by in October, all that remained was the stone chimney, some burnt

The left section of the Diamond Springs Pony Express Station was made of limestone slabs compacted with mud. The limestone slab of the station, which is on private property, is still visible from a country road on the west side of the Diamond Mountains. Nevada Historical Society, Reno, Nevada

wood, and buried bodies. Sometime later the station was rebuilt and served Holladay's Overland Stage and Mail Company.

When the westbound Pony rider came in to Egan, the conflict was over and the soldiers waiting for reinforcements were milling about. He changed horses and rode "hell bent for leather" to Butte station, then Mountain Springs, and on to the Ruby Valley station.

The Ruby Valley station was a welcome site. It had water and rich soil and fields of hay. Station attendants William "Uncle Billy" Rogers and Frederick William Hurst raised hay and some vegetables for the other Pony Express stations. In 1860 and 1861 soldiers camped at Ruby Valley and sent out detachments to protect stations and travelers east and west. In 1862 the Pony Express was no longer running, but hostilities still threatened overland passage. The army built Fort Ruby a couple of miles southeast of the Ruby Valley station as a base camp for their patrols protecting the Overland Stage traffic and telegraph lines from Indian attacks.

Years later the remnant of the Ruby Valley station was moved to the museum at Elko, Nevada, and the desert claimed the old fort.

It was a long, dry, twenty-two-mile ride over steep hillsides and through winding canyons from the Ruby Valley station to Diamond Springs, where the Pony Express rider could get a fresh horse. "The station is named Diamond Springs, from an eye of warm, but sweet and beautifully clear water bubbling up from the earth," wrote Sir Richard Burton in 1860, but Edna B. Patterson in the January 1960 *Nevada State Journal* claims the station was named for Jack Diamond, a prospector. The real source of the name may never be known, and the Diamond Springs station, like so many others, was eventually reclaimed by the desert.

It was nearly twenty miles to the home station at Robert's Creek and the last station in Egan's Division Four. The station was named for the Division Five superintendent, Boliver Roberts, possibly because he and Egan built it—twice.

In the second week of the Pony Express, a harbinger of trouble in the days to come occurred when a small party of Shoshone and Paiutes drove off the horses at the Robert's Creek station. A few weeks later the Paiute War began. Up and down the trail the stock was driven off, several station keepers killed, and some stations burned, including the Robert's Creek station.

By early June, still in the midst of hostilities, Roberts, Egan, and a crew of riders, station keepers, and stock tenders set out to rebuild and restock the destroyed stations along the trail to keep the Pony Express running. The burned Robert's Creek station was partially rebuilt by October when Sir Richard Burton made his journey to California. He wrote that at the Robert's Creek station "loitered several Indians of the White-Knife tribe, which boasts, like the old Sioux and the modern Flatheads, never to have stained its weapons with the blood of a white man. . . . These men attend upon the station, and herd the stock, for an occasional meal, their sole payment."

The winter of 1860–1861 was brutally cold and the snow deep. The Salt Lake City *Deseret News* reported in February 1861, "One Indian was recently found dead within a half mile of the (Robert's Creek) station, who had perished of cold and starvation while on his way there for food. Another had fallen down nearby from exhaustion, badly frozen, who was taken to the station and resuscitated before it was too late to save his life. Such a state of things among the red men is truly deplorable, but perhaps there is no way at present to ameliorating their condition."

Postcard showing Pony Bob Haslam making the fastest ride in the history of the Pony Express to deliver the election returns of Abraham Lincoln.

8

BRAVING THE DESERT, WAR, AND THE SIERRA NEVADA

> *Sacramento Daily Union*
> March 19, 1860
> MEN WANTED!
> The undersigned wishes to hire ten or a dozen men,
> familiar with the management of horses, as hostlers, or
> riders on the Overland Express Route via Salt Lake City.
> Wages $50 per month and found. I may be found at the St.
> George Hotel during Sunday, Monday and Tuesday.
> WILLIAM W. FINNEY

The westernmost division of the Pony Express was managed by two men—William W. Finney, the general agent of Pacific operations, and Boliver Roberts, the Division Five superintendent. Finney was put in charge of Pacific operations by Benjamin Ficklin, the general manager of the Pony Express. Ficklin and Finney were friends. They both attended Virginia Military Institute. Little is known about Finney before he went to work for the Pony Express, other than when asked he immediately boarded a ship to California and began establishing the western operations of the Pony Express. His arrival was announced in San Francisco on March 15, and on March 19 he placed an ad announcing that he was hiring hostlers and riders for the Overland Express Route. Four days later, on March 23, the newspapers reported that Finney had stocked the trail from Eagle Valley (Carson Valley)

Division Five superintendent Boliver Roberts managed the division from his headquarters in Carson City. Special Collections, J. Willard Marriott Library, University of Utah

to Sacramento and, "For express and pack service he has purchased one hundred and twenty-nine mules and horses—about a hundred of the latter. They are all California stock, and well adapted for riding and packing purposes. The necessary saddles for riding and packing, with bridles, blankets, etc. were purchased here and in San Francisco. A certain number of tents and tent poles were also provided for the use of the men who are stationed beyond Carson Valley. Twenty-one men, as express riders and packers, started with the train. The men and animals will be distributed between this city and Eagle Valley; the line to that point (from Roberts' Creek to Eagle Valley) is to be stocked from Salt Lake." It was an amazing four days work and typical of Finney's decisive capability to get things done.

When credit to finance the operations of the Pony Express started drying up, Finney was either granted the power or took it upon himself to persuade the future "Stagecoach King" Ben Holladay to accept drafts for operating capital to keep the western end of the line running. But despite Finney's value to Russell, Majors, and Waddell, and his proven capability to manage the operations of the Pony Express, his time with the company was cut short by the bigwigs of San Francisco and his own stubborn streak.

According to Roy Bloss in *Pony Express — The Great Gamble,* San Francisco newspapers began printing advance notices of the inbound Pony Express mail based on the list they received by wire from Carson City. The advance notice enabled commercial houses to act on anticipated incoming documents and money matters that affected their operations. Finney, for reasons he refused to explain, ordered the newspapers to stop the practice. As soon as word got around, eleven powerful San Francisco magnates publicly and privately protested Finney's decision and urged him to change his decision. Finney wouldn't budge. Thirteen days later, on September 19, 1860, Finney was unceremoniously replaced as general agent of the Pacific. He disappeared from the scene without fanfare and W. C. Marley, the Buckland's station keeper, took his place. According to Finney's great-great-granddaughter Beverly Johnson of Tennessee, Finney joined the Confederate Army and was caught smuggling guns for the South and imprisoned in New York. He managed to escape and get to New Orleans, where he caught a boat to Paris, France, and later sent for his family. Nothing else is known about him.

Roberts had his hands full responding to the flood of orders coming from the energetic Finney. His job was to see to it that the operations that Finney and he set up ran without a hitch — stock and supplies were always in place, riders were where they were supposed to be, and horses were at the ready. Roberts was a restless man from a restless family, but unlike Finney he stayed with the company for the entire period of the Pony Express.

As a child, Illinois-born Roberts moved from town to town around the Midwest with his doctor father, Daniel Roberts, his mother and brother William. They settled in Lancaster, Missouri, and stayed there a short time. At nineteen, Boliver saddled his horse, put a rifle in a scabbard and supplies in a saddlebag, and crossed the Great Plains to Provo, Utah. A year later, in 1851, his family joined him. Still restless, the Roberts men moved on to Placerville, San Jose, and San Bernardino — the elder Roberts practiced medicine, and the boys worked the mines. William and their father returned to Provo around 1853, but Boliver kept at it until 1854. Finally deciding that mining would not make him rich, he quit and took a job with the Mail and Express Company that ran from Salt Lake City to Carson City. Five years later he went to Dayton, Nevada, to build a bridge across the Carson River, and in 1860 he signed on with the Pony Express.

When the Pony Express stopped running, Roberts moved to Salt Lake City, married, fathered five children, and scouted for a time. Then he went on to become a partner in the Bassett and Roberts mercantile business, a contractor for the Central Pacific Railroad, a city councilman, director of the Utah Commercial and Savings Bank, and in 1866 was appointed treasurer of the Territory of Utah. Roberts died in 1893 in his Salt Lake City home.

The Paiute War

It was Finney, Roberts, and Division Four superintendent Howard Egan's unfortunate luck to have their first few months of operations confounded by the outbreak of the Paiute War. Desperate, angry Great Basin Paiutes, Goshutes, Shoshones, and Bannocks waged a war for survival, raiding and burning stations, killing station keepers and stock tenders, and pursuing Pony Express riders. It was the only time in the history of the Pony Express that the mail did not go through. Russell, Majors, and Waddell canceled Pony Express operations between Carson City and Salt Lake City in June 1860 for almost a month.

The war had been simmering for some time, but the event that ignited it into a bloody conflict between Indians and settlers occurred on May 7 at Williams station about ten miles east of Buckland's station near the Big Bend of the Carson River. On Tuesday morning, May 8, James O. Williams, who had been away all night, returned to his home at Williams station and found his two brothers, Daniel and Oscar, dead, and patrons of the Williams's makeshift saloon—Samuel Sullivan, James Fleming, and a man known only as Dutch Phil—were also dead. The house had been burned to the ground and the stock run off. Williams, terrified by the mutilation of the bodies he saw and what horrors may be lurking about, rode from the grim scene west toward Buckland's station as fast as his horse would take him.

The May 9 *Sacramento Daily Union* reported that Williams rode onto Buckland's station, saying that at least twelve or thirteen other whites had apparently also been murdered and, "The Indians are about five hundred strong and all mounted. They pursued him to within six miles of Buckland's and gave up the chase." Various reports went on to say that Williams then rode toward Virginia City, stopping on the way to warn the settlers at Dayton and Silver Springs that the Paiutes were on the warpath. The May 21 *New York Times* reported a different version, writing that seven miles down the road Williams "found one of the riders of the Pony Express, told him the news, with such embellishments as his fear suggested, and engaged him to ride into Virginia City with it." Coast to coast the alarm was sounded and a firestorm of fear and angry shouts for revenge spread throughout the frontier.

What really happened at Williams station is a mystery, but most historians agree that the Williams brothers or their cohorts were holding two Indian women captive in the root cellar under the barn. According to some accounts, the Indians may have been young girls of twelve or thirteen out gathering piñon nuts. Presumably the girls or women were raped. Their father and nine men came to their rescue, and in the fury of the attack tortured and killed the men, burned the station, and carried the girls away. They had had enough of the white man's treatment. The abuse of the two girls was the final blow.

An overlooked but equally convincing theory put forth in the *San Francisco Herald* claimed that the Williams station massacre was by whites. The author, bylined as "Tennessee," wrote that there were only three men and they were killed with an axe. Money was taken, but no food stores, and the stock were not run off. It was well known that the Indians were starving, and it was unlikely that they would attack and leave food behind, "facts strongly tending to show that the aborigines had nothing to do with this atrocious murder." Adding to the theory was the rumor that a worthless

Numaga, chief of Pyramid Lake Paiutes. Nevada Historical Society, Reno, Nevada

fellow named "Yank" and his companions were at Williams's saloon gambling. Yank lost all his money to the Williams brothers and, believing he had been cheated, killed them, took the money, and burned the house to cover his crime.

Meanwhile a large band of Paiutes and their Bannock and Shoshone allies were gathered in council at Pyramid Lake to powwow about their dire situation. They had suffered through a winter of fierce blizzards and were starving. There was no relief in sight from the juggernaut of settlers coming into their homelands, squatting near their water sources, hacking down the piñon pines, trampling the vegetation, and robbing them of their major sources of food—piñon nuts, roots, tubers, fish, and berries. Over the years many of the Indians had family who were killed or cruelly treated by the whites, and their bitter stories gnawed at their hungry bellies.

During council the majority of leaders chose war to drive the white invaders from their territory. Only Numaga of the Pyramid band of the Paiute spoke against war: "They will come like the sand in a whirlwind and drive you from your homes. You will be forced among the barren rocks of the north, where your ponies will die; where you will see the women and old men starve, and listen to the cries of your children for food."

Numaga argued for peace for three days, then the news of the attack at the Williams station reached the gathering, and he knew what would happen: "There is no longer any use for counsel; we must prepare for war."

At the time there were only a few U.S. troops in the territory. Among them was Major William O. Ormsby, who was already on his way to Pyramid Lake with an "expeditionary force" of 105 men, mostly volunteers from the saloons in Carson City, to exact revenge for the killings and teach the Indians a lesson. Poorly armed and more than a few drunk, the ragtag army rode into the canyon south of Pyramid Lake, where the Paiutes, Shoshone, and Bannocks easily picked them off, killing seventy-six, wounding many, and chasing the rest into the desert. The badly wounded Ormsby tried to surrender, but the Indians took no notice and shot him.

When news of Ormsby's military disaster reached Virginia City and Carson City and spread throughout the country, terrified settlers barricaded themselves inside their houses or packed up and left the territory. Virginia City suspended mining business for sixty days to prevent claim jumping. Some station keepers abandoned their posts, but most stayed and only one Pony rider refused to make his regular mail run.

Bob Haslam and a group of frontier entrepreneurs don their most distinguished pose for the camera. Left to right, standing, Pony Express rider Bob Haslam and dime-novel king Prentiss Ingraham; seated, J. B. Colton, Alexander Majors, and "Buffalo Bill" Cody.

The Perilous Trail

Pony Express riders making the run between Roberts Creek and Sacramento had to outrun Paiutes and Shoshones in the wastelands of the Great Basin and press their way through blinding blizzards in the rugged snowbound reaches of the high mountains of the Sierra-Nevada. It was tough going.

Adding to their hardships was the thirty-five- to forty-mile distance between some of the stations. The distance was longer than a good horse could maintain top speed. Fifteen months after the Pony Express started operating, more stations were built to shorten the overall Pony Express delivery time. These relays, such as Grubb's Well and Mount Airy or Dry Wells, didn't amount to much—just corrals and makeshift structures. They were a form of hell for the station tenders but provided the rider with a fresh horse.

Two days after the massacre at the Williams station and while Ormsby was leading his volunteers to Pyramid Lake, Pony rider Robert "Pony Bob" Haslam made the longest, most famous ride of the Pony Express.

Haslam was born in London, immigrated to America, and came to Utah Territory in his teens during the Mormon migration. He was twenty when Roberts hired him to build stations and make the seventy-five-mile Express run between Buckland's station east of Carson City and Friday's station at the southwest shore of Lake Tahoe.

On May 9, Haslam left Friday's station heading east. He rode into Carson City, heard the Paiutes were on the "warpath," then went on to Miller's station, where he discovered that the Carson City volunteers on their way to Pyramid Lake with Ormsby had taken all the Express horses. Haslam fed and watered his weary mount and rode on to Buckland's, where he and the horse could take a long rest. At Buckland's, station keeper W. C. Marley and relief rider Johnson Richardson were in "something of a panic." Richardson, in the vernacular of the time for cowardice, "dumped the blanket" and refused to ride. Marley offered Haslam a fifty-dollar bonus to take the ninety-mile run to Smith's Creek. Whether it was the promise of the fifty dollars or Haslam's sense of duty, he jumped into the saddle of a fresh horse and continued his run east through the Sink at Carson Springs and the alkali desert to Sand Springs, Cold Springs, and finally Smith's Creek. He had ridden 190 miles without rest. The exhausted Haslam climbed into a bunk and slept for eight hours. When the westbound *mochila* arrived, he leaped onto the saddle and headed back to Cold Springs. As he was galloping up to Cold Springs, he discovered the Paiutes had been there and had killed the station keeper and run off the stock. Haslam watered his horse, then rode on to Sand Springs. He told the lone stock tender at Sand Springs about the attack at Cold Springs and urged him to come along with him if he valued living. The tender took heed, and the two men rode west to the Sink of Carson station.

Envelope announcing Abraham Lincoln elected as president. Courtesy Colorado Historical Society (10027153)

Haslam proved to be right; the Sand Springs station was attacked the next morning. The station keepers at Sand Springs fought the Indians for four days from the shelter of the stone station until fifty volunteers from Cold Springs rode in scattering the Indians.

When Haslam and the stock tender pulled up at Carson Sink, they found fifteen frightened men barricaded in the adobe station. Some reportedly were survivors of the Pyramid disaster. Haslam rested for an hour, left the stock tender with the men at Carson Sink, and rode west to Buckland's station.

No one was more surprised or happy to see Haslam than Marley. In his delight he promised to double Haslam's bonus. There was still no relief rider at Buckland's, so Haslam rested for ninety minutes and then carried the mail to Carson City and on to his home station at Friday's. When he pulled up at Friday's, Haslam had ridden 380 miles in thirty-six hours. When later asked about the ride, he said, "I was rather tired, but the excitement of the trip had braced me up to stand the journey."

In November Haslam carried the news of Lincoln's election to Fort Churchill, and in March of the following year he carried Lincoln's inaugural address the 180 miles from Smith's Creek to Fort Churchill in eight hours and ten minutes. It was the fastest ride ever recorded by the Pony Express.

Long after the Pony Express quit running, Haslam kept riding. He was hired by Wells Fargo & Company to ride express mail between Virginia City and Friday's station in Nevada. Eight years later he traded riding express in the deserts of Nevada for a hundred-mile route between Queen's River and Owhyee River in Idaho. After several more years of hard riding, he traded his saddle for the driver's box of a stagecoach, driving Wells Fargo passengers the 720 miles between Salt Lake City and Denver. Haslam died at age seventy-two in Chicago.

A little over a week after Haslam made his 380 mile run to deliver the mail, the Dry Creek station was attacked.

As dawn broke through the open door of the Dry Creek station, John Applegate was stoking the cooking fire to make breakfast and Ralph Rosier was trudging toward the spring to get a bucket of water. "Bolly" Bolwinkle, the third man assigned to the station, was still deep in sleep when a rifle shot rang out followed by Rosier's agonizing cry of pain. Applegate ran to the door.

Rosier lay dying a few yards away, and Si McCandless, who owned the trading post across the road, was running toward the doorway. Another shot rang out. Applegate fell to the floor, shot in the groin. Bolwinkle, suddenly jerked out of his sleep by the gunfire, leaped out of his bed and he and McCandless stacked grain bags in the doorway and started firing back.

Sometime during the firefight Applegate asked for a gun. McCandless or Bolwinkle, thinking the wounded man wanted to help fight off the Indians, tossed him a pistol. Applegate urged Bolwinkle and McCandless to try to escape. When they refused to leave, Applegate, possibly knowing that he had no chance to survive his wounds, put a bullet through his own head.

As suddenly as the firing started, it stopped. McCandless, who had married a Paiute woman and had traded with her relatives for years, was convinced the Paiutes would not hurt him and talked Bolwinkle into making a run for the next station. A few Indians gave chase, then broke off and returned to loot the Dry Creek station. It's not clear where Bolwinkle and McCandless finally made it to safety. Had they reached the Simpson Park station, they would have found station keeper James Alcott dead and the station burned. Farther west, Jacob's Spring in the Reese

River Valley was burned. The Smith Creek station, some thirty miles farther, was not attacked, but still farther west the Indians had returned to the Cold Springs station and burned it.

During the concentrated attacks on the stations in May 1860, the Pony Express riders kept the mail moving, although station after station was burned, the hostlers and stock tenders killed or chased away, and the stock scattered, leaving the riders without fresh horses to speed them across the desert. Even their tired ponies didn't give up. When chased, these grain-fed runners

Remains of the Dry Creek station. Bart Smith

Smith's Creek Pony Express and Overland Stage Station between Dry Creek and Cold Springs station. UNRS-P1992-01-8497, James R. Herz Collection. Courtesy Special Collections, University of Nevada, Reno, Nevada

still outdistanced the grass-fed Indian ponies. But the damage to the stations and random attacks had the whole country in turmoil. In June Russell, Majors, and Waddell shut down mail delivery between Salt Lake City and Sacramento until

U.S. Army troops were dispatched to curb the attacks.

Meanwhile Finney had asked the army to send seventy-five soldiers to patrol the line from Carson City to Dry Creek. His request was denied, but it didn't stop Finney and Roberts from gathering up every man they could spare to start rebuilding the burned stations and get the Pony Express running again.

In July the U.S. Army built Fort Churchill about a mile from Buckland's station to establish a military presence in the area. The Indian attacks and military counter actions continued into August and September, then the Paiutes, Goshutes, and Shoshones appeared to give up

A "fog bow" over a Pony Express station west of Austin. Bart Smith

hope of driving the white man away. Hostilities subsided, but they did not cease.

Four months after the war, Sir Richard Burton was passing through on his journey west and spent an October night at Dry Creek. He found "the station on a grassy bend at the foot of low rolling hills. It was a mere shell, with a substantial stone corral behind, and the inmates were speculating upon the possibility of roofing themselves in before winter. Water is found in tolerable quantities below the station, but the place deserved its name, Dry Creek." After a "frugal feed," Burton and his companions inspected Rosier's and Applegate's graves, listened as the new station keeper told the story of the Indian attack, and spent a comfortable night "under the leeward side of a large haystack. The weather was cold, but clear and bright. We slept the sleep of the just."

Burton also found that the Simpson's Park station was being rebuilt, "a new building of adobe was already assuming a comfortable shape" at Reese River Valley, and farther west the Cold Springs station was being rebuilt with stone and "was a wretched place half built and wholly unroofed." The Sand Springs station had withstood the attacks but described by Burton in October as "roofless and chair less, filthy and squalid, with a smoky fire in one corner, impure floor, walls open to the wind, and the interior full of dust."

West of Cold Springs, the Pony Express rider followed the Mormon-California Trail, which bowed southwest at Middle Creek. He changed horses at Westgate, Sand Springs, Sand Hill, Carson Sink, Hooten Wells, Buckland's, and Fort Churchill and then rode northwest to Miller's station, where the trail headed nearly straight west again. During the last seven months of operations, the trail was changed to follow the nearly straight west "Stillwater Dogleg" route from Cold Springs. The Fairview, Mountain Well, Stillwater, Old River, Bisby's, Nevada, Ragtown, and Desert Wells stations served as relays. Both the old trail and the Stillwater Dogleg merged at Miller's station.

The original station at Carson Sink was probably a brush shelter built by Chorpenning for his mail route in 1859. In March 1860 Roberts and J. G. Kelly "began the erection of a fort to protect us from the Indians. As there were no rocks or logs in that vicinity, it was built of adobes, made from the mud on the shores of the lake. To mix this and get it to the proper consistency to mould into adobes, we tramped all day in our bare feet. This we did for a week or more and the mud being strongly impregnated with alkali carbonate of soda, you can imagine the condition of our feet. They were much swollen and resembled hams."

The stone remains of the Cold Springs station. The station was 116 feet by 51 feet and the walls six feet high and three feet thick. There were four rooms—storage area, living quarters and a barn and corral. The horse barn and corral were next to the living quarters to keep the horses close and safe and ready for the next rider.
Bart Smith

Captain James Simpson's 1859 survey party rounding Carson Lake (Carson Sink) when it was full. Watercolor by Henry von Beckh, who accompanied the survey party. Courtesy National Archives

In October, when Burton stopped at Carson Sink, "there was a frame house inside an adobe enclosure, and a pile of wood and a stout haystack promised fuel and fodder. The inmates however were asleep, and it was ominously long before a door was opened. At last appeared a surly cripple, who presently disappeared to arm himself with his revolver." Burton went on to write, "The judge asked civilly for a cup of water, he was told to fetch it from the lake which was not more than a

half miles they might chance to gather some. ". . . never did I see men so tamely bullied; they threw back the fellow's sticks, and cold, hungry, and thirsty simply began to sulk. An Indian standing by asked $20 to herd the stock for a single night. At last George, the Cordon Blue, took courage, so he went for water while others broke up a wagon plank, and supper after a fashion was concocted."

After several battles during the Paiute War, the U.S. Army ordered Captain Joseph Stewart's Carson River Expedition to build a military post on 1,384 acres adjacent to Buckland's Ranch on the banks of the Carson River. Stewart began construction on July 20, 1860. The outpost was the largest cavalry post in the far West, garrisoning two thousand men. The adobe fort also housed the Pony Express station in its headquarters.

Northwest of Fort Churchill was Miller's and then Dayton and Carson City. These stations were used by the Overland Stage and Pony Express but were originally built to provide California-bound pioneers with supplies and a rest stop before tackling the Sierra Nevada Mountains. The towns prospered in 1849 when gold was discovered in Gold Canyon and boomed in 1859 when the main vein of the Comstock Lode was discovered.

mile off, though as the road was full of quagmires it would be hard to travel at night." The travelers offered to buy it or borrow it and replace it in the morning, but the station keeper told them to go for it themselves and that after about two and

Remains of officer's quarters at Fort Churchill. Fort Churchill is now a Nevada State Historic Park eight miles south of Silver Springs on US 95. Bart Smith

West of Carson City, in the foothills of the Sierra Nevada, stood the Mormon settlement of Genoa founded by John Reese in 1849. "Not a single white man was there then. The nearest white man was a man in Gold Canyon who had a trading post there before and he wintered there in a kind of small dug-out." (The trader in Gold Canyon was nicknamed "Virginia." and the

Mormon Station Historic Park. Genoa Pony Express Station was across the street. Bart Smith

mining boomtown of Virginia City was named for him.) "The first thing that I done when I got there was to get a ranche just where I thought was the best place and I built a house and it was called the 'Mormon station.'" The trail west from Genoa connected with a road built by Californians across the Sierra Nevada that was used as a mail route to the Nevada mining camps.

When John Reese founded Genoa at the base of the Sierra Nevada Mountains, the trail from Camp Floyd west of Salt Lake City followed the northerly Humboldt River and was the primary route of emigrants to California. In 1859 Captain James H. Simpson of the Corps of Engineers surveyed a southerly route across the Great Basin. Six weeks after he set out from Camp Floyd, he reached Genoa, calculating he had cut 288 miles off the Humboldt River route. In the years following, California-bound emigrants, freighters, the overland "Jackass" mail service, and the Pony Express used Simpson's shortcut.

Braving the Sierra Nevada

In winter the tortuous trail from Genoa across the Sierra Nevada was the worst stretch of trail of the entire 1,966-mile Pony Express route. The trail was steep, and the passes were snowbound half the year. For the first month of Pony Express operations, the trail from Genoa followed the roundabout Mormon Carson Emigrant Trail along the ridge of the Sierra's crest to Woodford's in the Carson Valley, then went westward through Luther's Pass and over Echo Summit. By the middle of May, the Pony riders were taking the shorter, more direct route straight up the Kingsbury Grade toll road through Daggett Pass and over the crest of the Sierra Nevada to Friday's station on the shores of Lake Bigler, later known as Lake Tahoe.

Friday's, operated by Martin K. "Friday" Burke and James Washington Small, was the last station on the trail before crossing into California. It was not operating as a Pony Express station until May, when the riders started using the Kingsbury Grade shortcut. Then its large log cabin, two-and-a-half-story hostelry, dining room, kitchen, storeroom, woodshed, and large stable and hay barn became the home station of legendary riders "Pony Bob" Haslam and Warren "Boston" Upson.

Pony riders generally agreed that a run through the mountains "in a blizzard in sub-zero cold with snowdrifts higher than a man's head" was worse than fending off Indian attacks, crossing oven-hot deserts, and fording raging rivers.

Pony Express statue located outside Harrah's Casino at South Lake Tahoe, about a mile west of the former location of Friday's Station. The statue is a National Pony Express Trail Marker dedicated April 4, 1963. Courtesy Nevada State Library and Archives, Nevada National Guard Photo Collection, Carson City, Nevada

Crossing the Sierras in a snowstorm. Sketch from
Hutchings' California Magazine, July 1860. Courtesy California History Room,
California State Library, Sacramento, California

On the inaugural run of the Pony Express from Sacramento east to St. Joseph, the fine California weather of the previous three weeks had turned cold and stormy, and by the time the rider from Sacramento handed the mail pouch over to Upson at Sportsman's station to carry over the Sierra Nevada to Mormon station in Genoa, sheets of falling rain had made a quagmire of the trail. The farther east he rode, the worse the storm became—the rain turned to snow and hail driven by fierce winds pelted his face. The trail was covered with snow and piling deeper every minute. He pushed on, changing horses at Moss relay, then crossed Anthony Brockliss's snow-covered bridge over the American River. Struggling through the relentless storm, he urged his storm-battered pony on to Webster's relay, then on to Strawberry and Lake Valley relays. At the Strawberry station, Upson's boss, Boliver Roberts, was waiting with a string of mules to help him through the snowstorm on Echo Summit. Just what Upson, Roberts, and the mules did is not recorded, but we do know that Upson pressed on through the blinding snowstorm, finally reaching Mormon station at Genoa. Wet, cold, hungry, and exhausted, he passed the eastbound mail to the next rider. A week later he made the westbound run in a blinding snowstorm, coming upon a string of snow-stranded pack mules that were left in the narrow trail below Echo Summit. He couldn't pass the mules without tumbling over the edge. He got off his horse and dug a path around each mule, finally making his way past the string three and half hours later. He then headed west toward Sportsman's station with the first westbound mail.

After the Pony Express started using the Kingsbury Grade shortcut over the Sierra Nevada

Miner's cabin in the Sierra Nevada Mountains. Library of Congress, Prints and Photographs Division

Mountains, westbound Pony riders leaving Friday's on the shore of Lake Bigler rode southwest, changed horses at Fountain Place and Yank's, and crossed the spine of the Sierra Nevada at Echo Summit before making their run to the home station at Sportsman's Hall.

Sportsman's Hall, also known as Twelve Mile (from Placerville) station, was one of the few stations where Pony riders enjoyed their stay. Brothers John and James Blair provided comfortable rooms and fine food—luxuries Pony riders seldom experienced.

**Above, Sportsman's Hall
Pony Express Station.**
Courtesy Society of California Pioneers,
San Francisco, California

Right, plaque commemorating the Pony Express outside
restaurant, which once was
Sportsman's Hall station.
Bart Smith

THE PONY EXPRESS

SACRAMENTO · FRIDAY'S   SACT. · LAKE CITY   JULESBURG   FT. KEARNY   ST. JOSEPH
                                                                    MARYSVILLE
                                                FT. LARAMIE

1860 : 1861

SPORTSMAN'S HALL
CALIFORNIA'S ONLY HOME STATION WHERE RIDERS
CHANGED ON THE PONY EXPRESS TRAIL. HERE,
AT 8:01 A.M. ON APRIL 4, 1860, SAM HAMILTON,
FIRST EASTBOUND RIDER, WAS RELIEVED BY
WARREN UPSON WHO CARRIED THE INITIAL
MAIL OVER THE THEN STORM SWEPT SIERRAS.

1960 : 1961

NATIONAL PONY EXPRESS CENTENNIAL ASSOCIATION
DWIGHT D. EISENHOWER — CHAIRMAN   WADDELL F. SMITH — PRESIDENT

The relief rider, leaving the comfort of Sportsman's near the base of the Sierra Nevada Mountains, descended toward the low hills and ravines to Louis Lepetit's station in the gold rush town of Placerville on the banks of Hangtown Creek. By 1860 Placerville had a telegraph office that connected with Sacramento and San Francisco. Riders picked up telegrams to be carried east and left telegrams to be transmitted west.

The raucous mining settlement was first known as Ravine City and sometimes as Old Dry Diggings, then Hangtown, and finally Placerville. These names, however unintended, tell its history. The 1848 mining camp called Ravine sprouted in the narrow ravines at the base of the Sierra Nevada Mountains, where swift streams flowed and then slowed and relinquished their treasure of gold. A year later nearly ten thousand men were swarming the hillsides carrying picks and gold pans—the basic tools of their trade. The luckless and the ones who had to haul in water to pan their diggings dubbed the settlement and its surroundings "Old Dry Diggings." Sometime during 1849 the camp became known as Hangtown. There are several versions of the event that earned the town this name. One is that three men were in a tent saloon at Old Dry Diggings playing poker. "In due time one of the party got 'broke.'" The loser in the card game suggested to his companions that the proprietor, who was asleep at the time, had gold dust stashed away and their game could be profitably continued if they relieved the saloon owner of his gold dust. One of them put a pistol to the saloon keeper's head, convincing him to tell them where the gold dust was hid. Then, with the dust in hand, they continued to play poker. The next day the saloon keeper mustered the courage to tell the camp about the robbery. The three men were arrested, tried in "miner's court," and sentenced to be flogged and run out of town. The sentence was immediately carried out. But a couple of days later, two of the scoundrels were liquored up and back in camp threatening the men who sentenced and flogged them. The miner's court met again, promptly arrested the two men, and hung them on "the leaning oak tree in the hay yard below Elstner's El Dorado Saloon, the same tree on which afterwards other malefactors expiated their crimes." Another oft-told story is that five outlaws of the Owls Gang robbed a French trading post and were caught and sentenced to be flogged thirty-nine times. After the flogging, three of the men were identified as wanted for murder on the Stanislaus River. Miner's court met again, tried the culprits, and hung them on an oak tree at Elsner's Hay Yard beside Hangtown Creek.

Main Street, early Placerville, California. Courtesy Society of California Pioneers, San Francisco, California

In the 1850s the citizens of Hangtown gave themselves the more respectable name of Placerville. Placerville was indeed a suitable name for a town founded on placer mining. The new name stuck, but Placerville never lost its earlier moniker of Hangtown and both names are used even today.

The Pony rider racing out of Placerville toward Sacramento during the first several months of operation rode the southerly White Rock Road, changing horses at El Dorado, which was also known as Mud Springs, Mormon Tavern, and Fifteen Mile House. Later they took a northerly route, relaying at Pleasant Grove, also known as Duroc and Folsom, before riding into the Five Mile station and on to Sacramento.

Sacramento was the finish line for westbound Pony Express riders during the first three months of operations. The Pony Express office was in the B. F. Hastings Building on the corner of Second and J Streets. On July 1 the Pony Express began using the first commercial railway in the

West—the 1856 twenty-two-mile-long Sacramento Valley Railroad between Folsom and Sacramento—to transport the mail. The finish line for Pony Express riders was then twenty-two miles shorter, and the Pony Express office in the Fol-

Pleasant Grove. Bart Smith

som Wells Fargo building became the end of the trail. In June 1861 Placerville became the western end of the trail, shortening the Pony Express relay even more.

Sacramento City, at the confluence of the

The B. F. Hastings Building in Sacramento housed Hastings's Bank and the Wells, Fargo & Company and Pony Express office. Library of Congress, Prints and Photographs Division

Sacramento and American Rivers, had been the hub of California's road system since the 1850s and the river port linking inland California to San Francisco. The bustling town of nearly fourteen thousand was a hive of busy activity. When the Pony Express rider came galloping in, the townspeople gathered outside the Wells Fargo office and eagerly awaited news from the east. They gathered again, twice a day—in the morning when the boat came in from San Francisco and in the evening when the outbound steamer departed. The docks were filled with stagecoaches picking up and letting off passengers and crowds of people milling about delivering or receiving parcels, exchanging news and pleasantries, and getting the latest news from San Francisco. Some of Sacramento's citizenry turned out just to join in the excitement of the hour. The *mochila* of mail was put aboard the steamboat and floated down the Sacramento River to the city on the bay, where a similar crowd of excited citizens gathered around the wharf waiting for the steamboat carrying the mail that had been relayed, pony by pony, rider by rider, across 1,966 miles of the great expanse that once separated them from the states in the East.

Early Sacramento. Note the telegraph lines along the left side of the street. California History Room, California State Library, Sacramento, California

Photograph of painting by George M. Ottinger. Courtesy Nebraska State Historical Society

Pony rider waves his hat to the men constructing the telegraph line that would soon span the continent and replace the Pony Express.

9

THE END AND THE MYTH

Samuel Morse's 1844 experimental telegraph line proved a great success, and by 1860 telegraph lines covered most of the United States east of the Missouri River. On the Pacific coast small telegraph companies in California had strung telegraph lines between San Francisco, Sacramento, and as far east as Carson City. The same want for faster communication between East and West that birthed the Pony Express drove Congress to pass the Pacific Telegraph Act of 1860 to "facilitate communication between the Atlantic and Pacific States by Electric Telegraph."

In 1861 a consortium of telegraph companies made up of the Western Union Company, and two fledgling California companies pulled together the necessary men, poles, wagon teams, and wire to build the line from Omaha, Nebraska, to Carson City. Holes were dug, poles were dropped, and wire was strung. The "trail of the wires" between the East and the West was roughly the same as the trail of the Pony Express. The line from the East reached Salt Lake City on October 18, 1861, and the line from Carson City reached Salt Lake City on October 24. The continent was spanned with wire, and the first coast-to-coast telegram was dispatched congratulating President Lincoln on the completion of the line and pledging California's continuing loyalty to the Union.

Two days later the Central Overland Company gave the order to stop the Pony Express. However, riders continued making local runs until November 20, 1861, when the last rider on the last run handed over the last mail by Pony Express.

Long before the telegraph reined in the Pony Express, the company that had set the "Greatest Enterprise of Modern Times" in motion was already collapsing. William Russell's financial shenanigans got the better of him, and a string of unfortunate events rolled Russell, Majors, and Waddell's corporate empire into bankruptcy.

The Pony Express was never a paying proposition, and Russell knew it wouldn't be — the company lost sixteen dollars on every piece of mail delivered. He counted on profits from the passenger stage operations and gambled that his company would get the overland fast-mail contract and a generous government subsidy once he proved the central route was passable in winter. He convinced his partners to take the risk. Meanwhile the company was stacking up huge debts.

On the verge of bankruptcy, Russell was desperate to get loans or credit to keep the stage line and Pony Express operating until the anticipated government subsidy came through. In a series of missteps, Russell became embroiled in a bond scheme that was his undoing.

A longtime friend and business associate introduced Russell to law clerk Godard Bailey, who was custodian of bonds belonging to the Indian Trust Fund managed by the Department of the Interior. Russell, with the approval of war secretary John B. Floyd, borrowed the bonds to use for collateral for short-term bank loans. Before Russell could pay off the bank loans and replace the bonds, the bonds were sold and consequently discovered missing from the Indian Trust Fund. Russell was arrested on December 24 and spent Christmas in a Washington jail. In January he was brought before a congressional committee for receiving stolen property and conspiring to defraud the government. Russell, Bailey, and Floyd were indicted but never tried. Floyd resigned his post as secretary of war and went south to join the Confederacy. Russell escaped prosecution on a technicality, and Bailey simply refused to answer his summons and was eventually forgotten, as Washington turned to face the problems of war. Sometime later the government reimbursed the trust fund. Russell walked away free, but the bond scandal damaged the reputation of the once-famous and respected firm of Russell, Majors, and Waddell beyond recovery and sealed its financial doom.

Adding to the company's woes was the near-fatal blow to their lucrative freighting business that had kept Russell, Majors, and Waddell's firm afloat since 1855 — they were underbid by another freighting company for a large part of the army's business.

A month after Russell's committee hearing on the bond scandal, Congress was in the process of approving an appropriations bill to provide a one-million-dollar-a-year subsidy for daily mail service across the central part of the continent. While the bill was being debated on the Senate floor, Confederate forces halted Butterfield's Overland Mail movement over the southern route. A hasty amendment to the bill switched Butterfield's operations to the central route and eliminated competitive bidding, shattering any chance Russell, Majors, and Waddell had to recover their losses. Not all was well for John Butterfield either. The year before, he was ousted from his own company for failing to pay debts he owed Wells Fargo & Company.

Russell, the entrepreneurial gambler, had one more card to play. His company had relay stations, Concord coaches, drivers, riders, and livestock that Butterfield's Overland Mail Company, owned by Wells Fargo & Company, needed to fulfill its government contract. In March 1861 Russell struck a deal to relinquish the western half of his stage and Pony Express route and trade the stations, men, and stock to Wells Fargo's Butterfield Overland Mail Company. In exchange, the two companies would split the mail subsidy and each pay for and control Pony Express operations

on its half of the route. This last gamble didn't work out quite the way Russell had planned. Even with a share of the government subsidy, Russell, Majors, and Waddell couldn't pay off their enormous debts. In March 1862 stagecoach king Ben Holladay, who had been quietly loaning them money for years, took over the company.

It was the end of the three most famous names on the frontier of the 1850s—Russell, Majors, and Waddell. Waddell went home to Lexington, Missouri, sold his home to his son for a dollar, and continued to live there until his death in 1872. Russell, at forty-eight, tried a comeback as a stockbroker in New York, but the bond scandal had left its mark and bankers and financiers refused to see him. For the once-great financial wizard, it was all downhill. Broke and humiliated, he sent letters pleading to Waddell and Majors for money, but they didn't have it to give. Eventually the man who was at his best making deals in boardrooms over brandy and fine cigars was reduced to living in shabby boardinghouses and selling Tic Sano, a patent medicine that claimed to cure neuralgia. At age sixty his family, whom he had essentially abandoned years before in his quest to become who he once was, brought him back to Missouri to die.

Majors started up a small freighting business,

The nation commemorates the Pony Express's 80th and 100th anniversaries.

but he gave it up after a string of unprofitable seasons. No stranger to hard work, he graded roadbed for the Union Pacific and tried prospecting. He moved from town to town and was finally found by his former employee, "Buffalo Bill" Cody, living alone in a mining shack outside of Denver writing his memoirs. Cody encouraged the old frontiersman to complete his memoirs of *Seventy Years on the Frontier* and paid for his keep while he finished writing the book. Cody also arranged to have it published. Majors's remaining days were spent remembering, as historian Christopher Corbett put it, "when he and his partners risked everything, when they put a little lad on the back of a horse named Sylph to cross the wide Missouri and streak west."

Memories and Myths

The Pony Express is the stuff of legend—the inspiring memory of a lone rider battling the elements and racing time to unite a nation. The Pony riders of our imagination were in fact courageous men of their word who let no element of man or nature stop them from speeding messages across the wild expanse of the American West. When they passed into history on November 20, 1861, these gritty riders had served their country well

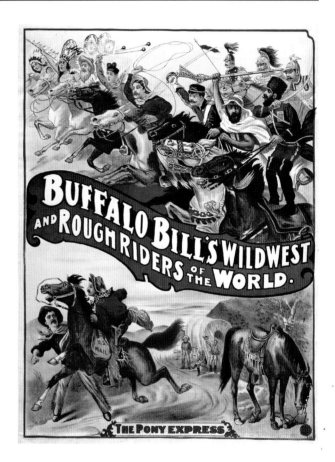

Poster advertising Buffalo Bill's Wild West Show featuring Teddy Roosevelt's Rough Riders and the Pony Express. Buffalo Bill Historic Center, Cody, Wyoming

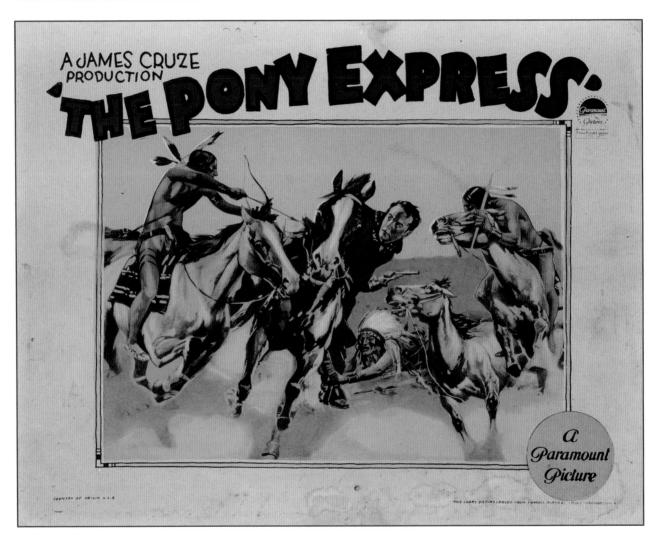

Ad for one of the many Pony Express films that captivated the imaginations of movie-goers.

during a critical time in our history and left a cherished legacy.

A decade after they quit running, the riders of the Pony Express galloped out of the 1860s and onto pages penned by Mark Twain as the "swift phantom of the desert." In the years that followed, their hard days in the saddle took on near-mythical rank as the heroes of dime-novel kings Ned Buntline's and Prentiss Ingraham's thrilling stories. The phantoms of the desert rode again in the 1880s and into the new century, crossing the continent and the ocean with Buffalo Bill's Wild West show. These representative Pony Express riders—some actually had been riders—represented the indomitable spirit of Americans to the world. Alexander Majors wrote their story in the 1890s, and in the early 1900s William Lightfoot Visscher thrilled readers with his account of Pony Express adventures on the trail. Countless others have told the story of the Pony Express since. In 1907 and into the 1950s, larger-than-life Pony Express riders streaked across the screen of movies and television shows. Today Pony riders show up at rodeos, parades, and amusement parks, and some linger around the old relay stations waiting to see who comes by.

We treasure the memory of the riders of the Pony Express, the truths, the myths, the legends, and sometimes we pretend we are them.

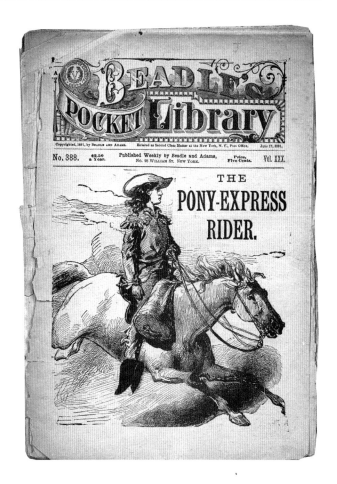

Cover of 1891 magazine featuring "Buffalo Bill" as "The Pony-Express Rider." Rare Books Division, The New York Public Library, Astor, Lenox and Tilden Foundations.

Courtesy of the Nevada State Library and Archives, Nevada National Guard Photo Collection, Carson City, Nevada

Pony Express Rider's Medal given to the riders of the 100th anniversary re-ride.

10

KEEPING THE SPIRIT ALIVE

*I*n the lingering aura of a vanished time, we still hear the hoof beats of the spirited ponies and see the sweat-stained faces of the riders and the rugged trail they rode long ago. Even from the distance of 150 years, the daring lone rider racing across the plains is the quintessential symbol of the spirit of the American West—and that spirit lives on.

In 1935 a group of riders leaped into their saddles to reenact the ride of the Pony Expressmen in celebration of the seventy-fifth anniversary. Five years later, the U.S. Postal Service launched a special ceremony commemorating the eightieth anniversary of mail service by Pony Express. In 1960 the Western Pony Express Trails Association joined the Central Overland Pony Express Trails Association to form the National Pony Express Centennial Association. The first order of business was to conduct a centennial re-ride so that America could once again hear the pounding hoof beats of the ponies speeding along the Pony Express Trail and recall that long-ago time.

Fascination with the Pony Express never waned; it has grown stronger with the passing of years. In 1978 a group of California trail riders organized the National Pony Express Association, and by 1980 the association had divisions in all eight states where the Pony Express trail traversed—Missouri, Kansas, Nebraska, Colorado, Wyoming, Utah, Nevada, and California. In 1992 Congress designated the trail a National Historic Trail. Nearly every spring since, usually in June, the riders of the National Pony Express Association mount up and re-ride the trail from St Joseph, Missouri, to Sacramento, California. The logistics of

A post designates the route of the Oregon, Mormon, California, and Pony Express Trails east of Granger, Wyoming. Bart Smith

the ride offer the National Pony Express Association challenges of a vastly different nature than those faced long ago by Russell, Majors, and Waddell. The organizers of the commemorative rides no longer face the problems of weather, bandits, and Indian attacks; instead they encounter the problems of high-speed automobile traffic in major cities and the logistics of arranging a clear path through busy towns and privately owned, sometimes fenced portions of the trail. Every year they take to the trail, the National Pony Express Association re-ride committee masterfully coordinates the event and robust crowds gather along the route to cheer the riders just as they did long ago.

The year 2010 marks the 150th anniversary of the Pony Express and of the time when this country was young and brave men and strong-hearted mustangs helped link the nation. Twenty-first-century Pony Express riders in the eight states of the Pony Express Trail will take to the trail in 2010 to commemorate the event.

APPENDIX A: FAST FACTS

Days of the Pony Express

- April 3, 1860, to November 20, 1861 (19 months)
- First westbound run:
    - o Departed St. Joseph, Missouri, on April 3, 1860, 7:15 p.m.
    - o Arrived in Sacramento, California, on April 13, 1860, 5:25 p.m.
    - o Arrived by steamer in San Francisco, California, on April 14, 1860, 12:38 a.m.
- First eastbound run:
    - o Departed San Francisco by steamer on April 3, 1860, 4:00 p.m.
    - o Departed Sacramento on April 4, 1860, 2:45 a.m.
    - o Arrived in St. Joseph on April 14, 1860, 1:00 a.m.
- West- and eastbound riders passed each other on April 8, west of Farson, Wyoming (place and date calculated by historians).
- The mail only failed to go through during the Indian uprisings, when Pony Express operations were suspended from May to late June 1860.
- U.S. Transcontinental Telegraph line completed on October 24, 1861
- Official Central Overland California and Pikes Peak Express Company order to stop Pony Express operations: October 26, 1861
- Last official run of a Pony Express rider: November 20, 1861

Trail of the Pony Express

- Length of the trail: St. Joseph to San Francisco — 1,966 miles

- The length of 1,966 miles is the distance generally accepted as measured and reported by most historians. However, a GPS measurement by Joseph Nardone of the Pony Express Trails Association indicates the original trail was 1,943 miles.
- The length of the trail changed several times as alternate routes were opened to avoid difficult climbs and telegraph lines progressed eastward and westward, shortening the distance between Pony Express terminal points.

Mail Delivery Times

- The advertised delivery time and during the first months of operation: average of ten days
- During Indian uprising: various, depending on situation
- During winter weather: twelve to sixteen days
- Overall average (as calculated by Pony Express historian Joseph Nardone): twelve to thirteen days.

Cost of Mail

- Five dollars for a half-ounce piece of mail during the first months of operation. Later the price was reduced to $2.50 and eventually to $1.00. The price charged was at a significant loss to the company.

Pony Riders

- Eighty to one hundred riders were hired to run the mail between St. Joseph, Missouri, and Sacramento, California (the mail was delivered by steamboat between Sacramento and San Francisco). Some quit, some died, and others were hired in their place. One hundred fifty to well over two hundred names have been listed as riders during the nineteen months of the Pony Express; not all have been officially confirmed as Pony riders.

- Riders rode day and night as fast as conditions permitted. (The rides were not always at a full gallop as has often been reported.)
- Each rider rode seventy-five to one hundred miles, changing horses every eight to fifteen miles, depending on terrain and location of relay stations. During the early months of the Pony Express, some riders, especially those in the far West, changed horses every twenty-five to forty miles, depending on where relay stations had been located. As more relay stations were added to the line, the miles between a change of horses shortened.

Riders' Pay

- Averaged one hundred dollars a month plus room and board.

Horses

- Four hundred to five hundred horses were purchased for the Pony Express and distributed along the trail.

Stations

- Number of home stations: 25
- Number of relay stations: 88 to 159
- The number of stations operating at any one time changed frequently as stations were added to reduce the distance between relays and other stations were added or abandoned as routes changed and telegraph lines progressed.

APPENDIX B: PONY EXPRESS THEN AND NOW

Americans longing to reach back and touch their heritage and visitors from around the world with a desire to experience the American Old West drive, bicycle, hike, and ride the national historic trails in ever-increasing numbers. Some travel parts of the Oregon, California, and Mormon Pioneer Trails using handcarts and covered wagons to more closely parallel what the pioneers experienced. Many take to the trail on horseback, following the path of the Pony riders to partly experience the western landscape as those long-ago riders did. Most drive the trails, where it is still possible.

Fortunately for these heritage-seeking travelers and Old West enthusiasts, the trail of the Pony riders that crosses the present-day states of Missouri, Kansas, Nebraska, Wyoming, Utah, Colorado, Nevada, and California has been designated the Pony Express National Historic Trail. Although most of the stations have disappeared, the trail and station sites are identified by wayside exhibits or granite monuments, steel posts, and other commemorative markers. The interpretive exhibits along the trail provide interesting bits of history. The exhibits, the sites, the surrounding landscapes, and a little imagination provide an unforgettable step back in time.

The trail and historic sites are managed by cooperative agreement between federal and state agencies, public and private organizations, and private landowners and volunteers.

The National Park Service (NPS) publishes a map of the Pony Express National Historic Trail. In recent years the NPS has also published a series of National Historic Trails Interpretive Auto-Tour Guides, which provide driving directions to and along the Pony Express Trail and to the Pony Express sites. The guides also include the historic sites of the Oregon, California, and Mormon Pioneer Trails. They are available at most Oregon Trail, California Trail, and Pony Express Trail museums and gift shops and online at www.nps .gov/cali/planourvisit/brochures.

Among the many interesting sights along the Pony Express Trail are the stations that are still standing in whole or in part and can be visited or viewed 150 years later. Historical and twenty-first-century photographs of these stations are included throughout this book, and a list of their current operations follows.

Pony Express Stations Still Standing, Restored, or Re-created

Missouri

St. Joseph Pony Express Station/Patee House

Now the Patee House Museum at 1202 Penn St. in St. Joseph. Owned and operated by the Pony Express Historical Association. Features reconstructed offices of Russell, Majors, and Waddell. Holds commemoration of start of Pony Express in April and events in June to honor the annual re-ride of the Pony Express by members of the National Pony Express Association.

St. Joseph Pikes Peak/Pony Express Stables

Now the Pony Express National Museum at 914 Penn St. in St. Joseph.
The museum contains Pony Express exhibits and provides guided and self-guided tours, educational materials, and National Park Service auto-tour guides and maps.

St. Joseph Riverfront Ferry Landing

This former ferry landing for boats crossing the Missouri River and carrying emigrants bound for Oregon and California and Pony Express riders relaying mail between St. Joseph and San Francisco is now part of the St. Joseph Riverfront Park. Includes Pony Express monuments and interpretive displays.

Kansas

Marysville Pony Express Barn

The restored stone Pony Express Barn now operates as a privately owned museum at 106 South Eighth St. in Marysville. A Pony Express monument is located along US 36 west of Marysville.

Hollenberg Road Ranch, Pony Express Relay, and Overland Stage Station
This station, constructed in 1857, was the last station in Kansas. Hollenberg is the only original unaltered Pony Express station still standing. It now operates as part of the seven-acre Kansas State Park and is designated a National Historic Landmark. The park includes a museum, nature trails, a picnic area, interpretive markers, and monuments.

Nebraska

Rock Creek Pony Express Relay and Overland Stage Station
A reconstructed Rock Creek Pony Express station is now part of the Rock Creek Station State Historical Park. The 350-acre park, three miles northeast of Endicott, Nebraska, features Pony Express exhibits, pioneer graves, trail ruts, and emigrant trail– and Pony Express–era buildings.

Fort Kearny
The first military post in the West, Fort Kearny was established to protect emigrants on the Oregon Trail and served as a Pony Express and Overland stage stop. Reconstructed buildings are now part of Fort Kearny State Historical Park at 1020 V Rd., south of Kearney. It includes a Pony Express–era interpretive center and artifacts.

Willow Island Pony Express Relay
The original Willow Island Pony Express station was relocated to the Veterans Memorial Park at 104 East Ninth St. in Cozad and is open to the public.

Machette's Pony Express Station or Cottonwood Springs Pony Express Station
Historians differ on whether the 1860s-era cabin now standing in a Gothenburg city park was indeed a Pony Express station and whether it was Machette's or the Cottonwood Springs station. Regardless of its yet-to-be-confirmed history, the cabin is typical of the stations of the Pony Express. The building serves as a Pony Express Museum.

Ficklin's Springs/Ash Hollow Pony Express Relay Station
The station has disappeared, but the site is part of the Ash Hollow State Historical Park. The park protects over one thousand acres of historic trail and landscape. Park includes a visitor/interpretive center, exhibits, pioneer grave cemetery, cave, archeological exhibits, and ruts and swales of wagon trails.

Scotts Bluff/Fort Mitchell Pony Express Home and Overland Stage Station
The Pony Express station has disappeared, but the Scotts Bluff National Monument (two miles west of Gering) is a major historic trails museum and visitor center providing information about the Pony Express stations and the trail and artwork by pioneer artist William Henry Jackson.

Wyoming

Fort Laramie Pony Express Relay and Overland Stage Station
Now part of the Fort Laramie National Historic Site (965 Gray Rocks Rd., Fort Laramie). The buildings and grounds of the once-prominent army post are managed by the National Park Service and open to the public.

Fort Caspar/Guinard's/ Platte Bridge Station
Mormon pioneers crossed the Platte River near here in 1847. A small party of pioneers stayed to establish a ferry service. A trading post was built and later a toll bridge was also installed. This was also the site of a Pony Express station, and in 1862 the army established a military post at this location. An interpretive center now stands at the entrance of Fort Caspar. It provides historical displays, re-created buildings, on-site orientation, and self-guided tours.

Fort Bridger
The remaining and restored buildings of Fort Bridger are maintained as the Fort Bridger State Historic Park. The park contains a museum and provides exhibits and special tours and events commemorating the Mountain Men, the emigrants, and the Pony Express.

Utah

Carson Inn Pony Express Station near Camp Floyd in Fairfield

The Pony Express station was located in John Carson's Stagecoach Inn in Fairfield. The 1858 adobe building is still standing and is part of Utah State Park. It now has a wooden facade and is open to the public.

Simpson Springs Station

A number of structures were built in the area of Simpson Springs. Historians are not certain which served as the Pony Express station. A restored 1860s building is located on the Simpson Springs station site and may have been the station or an outbuilding of the station.

Boyd Pony Express Station

The Boyd station was a log structure. The stabilized ruins at the site include a one-room stone cabin with gun ports on all four sides that were used to protect the station keeper from robbers and Indian attacks.

Willow Springs Pony Express Home Station

The Pony Express monument and buildings of the home station are still standing. It is located on the westerly end of Callao and is the only existing home station maintained on private property.

Nevada

Cold Springs Station

The ruins of the thick stone walls with gun ports can be seen east of Middlegate. An interpretive sign on US 50 and a two-mile hike lead to the station ruins.

Sand Springs Station
Ruins of the Sand Springs station are now part of the Sand Springs Recreation Area west of Middlegate.

Fort Churchill Pony Express Station
The site is part of the Fort Churchill State Park at 1000 US 95A in Silver Springs. Some ruins of the fort remain. The park has a visitor center/museum, campgrounds, and picnic area.

Ruby Valley Pony Express Station
A reconstructed building of the Ruby Valley Pony Express station was relocated to the Northeastern Nevada Museum in Elko. The building and a Nevada State Historical Marker identify it as the Ruby Valley Pony Express station.

California

Sacramento Pony Express Home Station and Western Terminal of the Pony Express
The B. F. Hastings Building in Sacramento is the original structure that was located on the corner of Second and J Streets in Old Sacramento. Now the first floor of the building houses the Wells Fargo History Museum.

ADDITIONAL INFORMATION ABOUT THE TRAIL AND STATIONS

Pony Express National Historic Trail: www.nps.gov/poex

California National Historic Trail: www.nps.gov/cali

Mormon Pioneer National Historic Trail: www.nps.gov/mopi

Oregon National Historic Trail: www.nps.gov/oreg

Wyoming Tourism: www.wyomingtourism.org

Oregon and California Trails Association: www.octa-trails.org

Mormon Trail Association: www.mormontrails.org

National Pony Express Association: www.xphomestation.com

Pony Express Trail National Back Country Byway: www.utah.com/playgrounds/pony_ express

Great Basin National Heritage Route: www.greatbasinheritageorg/ponyexpress

Pony Express Territory: www.ponyexpressnevada.com

BIBLIOGRAPHY

Bloss, Roy S. *Pony Express — The Great Gamble.* San Diego: Howell-North Books, 1959.

Bradley, Glenn D. *The Story of the Pony Express.* Chicago: A. C. McClurg & Co., 1914.

Burton, Richard Francis. *The City of the Saints and Across the Rocky Mountains to California.* New York: Alfred A. Knopf, 1963.

Burton, Richard Francis. *The Look of the West, 1860: Across the Plains to California.* Lincoln, London: University of Nebraska Press, 1963.

Corbett, Christopher. *Orphans Preferred, The Twisted Truth and Lasting Legend of the Pony Express.* New York: Broadway Books, 2003.

Di Certo, Joseph J. *The Saga of the Pony Express.* Missoula, Montana: Mountain Press Publishing Company, 2002.

Dobbs, Hugh J. *History of Gage County, Nebraska.* Lincoln, Nebraska: Western Publishing & Engraving Company, 1918.

Egan, Howard. *Pioneering the West,1846-1878: Major Howard Egan's Diary.* Salt Lake City: Skelton Publishing Company, 1917.

Fike, Richard E., and John W. Headley. *The Pony Express Stations of Utah in Historical Perspective.* Salt Lake City: Bureau of Land Management, Utah, Cultural Resources Series, 1979.

Godfrey, Dr. Anthony. *Historic Resource Study Pony Express National Historic Trail.* La Crosse, Wisconsin: U.S. West Research, Inc. & U.S. Department of the Interior/National Park Service, August 1994.

Harley, William G. *Howard Egan, the Elkhorn Skirmish, and Mormon Trail Emigration in 1848.* Salt Lake City: Mormon Historic Site Foundation, Spring 2000.

Majors, Alexander. *Seventy Years on the Frontier.* Minneapolis: Ross & Haines, Inc., 1965.

Maurer, David A. "Pony Express Pioneer Left His Mark on VMI." Charlottesville, Virginia: *Charlottesville Daily Progress,* February 1993.

Nevin, David. *The Expressmen.* Chicago: Time-Life, Old West Series, 1974.

Reese, John. *Nevada Historical Society Papers 1913-1916, Vol. 1.* Carson City, Nevada: State Printing Office, 1917.

Root, Frank A., and William E. Connelley. *The Overland Stage to California.* Topeka, Kansas: Crane and Company, 1901 (reprinted by Long's College Book Company, Columbus, Ohio, 1950).

Root, George, and Russell K. Hickman, *Pike's Peak Express Companies.* Topeka, Kansas: *Kansas Historical Quarterly,* November 1945.

Settle, Raymond W., and Mary Lund, *Saddles and Spurs.* Harrisburg, Pennsylvania: Stackpole Co.,1955.

Twain, Mark. *Roughing It.* New York: Harper & Bros., 1872.

Whitney, Orson F. *History of Utah.* Salt Lake City: George Q. Cannon & Sons Co., October 1904.

INDEX

ABOUT THE AUTHOR

C. W. Guthrie is a freelance writer living in Montana with her husband, retired test pilot Joe Guthrie. She grew up unknowingly following the trail of the Pony Express as her family moved from mining town to mining town in the West. She has written five other books: *The First Ranger: Adventures of a Pioneer Forest Ranger — Glacier Country, 1902 to 1910*; *Glacier National Park Legends and Lore along the Going-to-the Sun Road*; *All Aboard for Glacier, The Great Northern Railway and Glacier National Park*; *Going-to-the-Sun Road and Glacier National Park's Highway to the Sky* (both recipients of the Association of Partners for Public Lands Award for a non-association published book); and *Glacier National Park: The First 100 Years* (recipient of the Benjamin Franklin Award for History).

ABOUT THE PHOTOGRAPHER

Photographer Bart Smith is hiking and photographing all of the national trails. His photographs have been published in such magazines as the *Smithsonian, National Geographic Adventure*, and *Backpacker*. His photographic books include *The Appalachian Trail: Calling Me Back to the Hills, Along the Pacific Crest Trail, Along the Florida Trail*, and *Along Wisconsin's Ice Age Trail*.